French
Political Parties

French
Political Parties

A Documentary Guide

edited by

N. A. ADDINALL

UNIVERSITY OF WALES PRESS
CARDIFF
1995

97-195027 (1)

British Library Cataloguing-in-Publication Data
A catalogue record for this book is available from
the British Library.

ISBN 0-7083-1263-2

Cover design by John Garland, Pentan Partnership, Cardiff
Typeset by Action Typesetting Ltd., Gloucester
Printed in Great Britain by Gwasg Dinefwr, Llandybïe

Contents

Preface vii

List of Contributors ix

Acknowledgements x

Part I: The Fifth Republic and its Constitution

Introduction to the constitution
N.A. ADDINALL 1

Part II: The Political Parties

General introduction to modern French political
parties
N.A. ADDINALL 28

1. Le Rassemblement pour la République
N.A. ADDINALL 35

2. L'Union pour la démocratie française
G.F. EVANS 47

3. Le Front national
C. RODGERS 67

4. Le Parti socialiste
N.A. ADDINALL 94

5. Le Parti communiste français
N.A. ADDINALL 120

6. Ecology parties in France
JUDITH K. PROUD 131

7. The trade unions
   N.A. ADDINALL   153

Appendices
   Appendix I: The presidents of the Fifth
      Republic   165
   Appendix II: The prime ministers of the
      Fifth Republic   166
   Appendix III: General election results
      1958–1993   167

Index   170

Preface

A week is most certainly a long time in politics and it is the reason why so many books on the subject can appear to be at least partially out of date by the time they appear in print. This is particularly the case for those which seek to detail and explain antagonisms or differences of opinion between politicians at a given point in time; what may have appeared to be important in a particular context may rapidly recede into insignificance and cease to have any major importance in the light of the development of subsequent events.

It is for this reason that my co-authors and I decided that a book on the Fifth French Republic needed primarily to provide the reader – academic, student, general reader – with essential information about how that Republic came into existence, how it developed, how its constitution works, how the fortunes of the different political parties have prospered and their ideas developed under it. To do this, we decided to devote chapters to the Fifth Republic and its constitution, to the different political parties and to the trade unions as well as providing factual information concerning presidents of the Republic, prime ministers and election results. What we have further tried to do is to provide the reader with illustrative texts, so that he/she can judge the information and ideas for himself/herself rather than accepting our analyses and suggestions at face value. This is why each explanatory chapter is accompanied, according to the subject, either by key articles from the constitution of the Fifth Republic or by detailed extracts from the published work of leading politicians of the right, centre and left, all of whom have given their permission for the reproduction of these extracts (headed 'Sources' in the text). At the same time, we have tried to help the reader examine these texts critically by providing lists of questions concerning them which should enable him/her to arrive at a personal reasoned judgement and we have also provided further subjects for discussion which should prove useful in pursuing lines of thought which the texts, the French politicians and our comments and questions may, we hope, inspire. Words shown in bold in the source texts are the subject of the questions which follow.

Our objective, therefore, has been to provide you, the reader, with a book which is both informative and thought-provoking and, in the hope of achieving that objective, we wish you *bonne lecture*.

N. A. ADDINALL
University of Wales, Swansea

The Contributors

Nigel Addinall is lecturer in French at the University of Wales, Swansea, and French Honorary Consul for Swansea and West Glamorgan.

George Evans is senior lecturer in French at the University of Wales, Swansea.

Judith Proud is principal lecturer in French at the University of Portsmouth.

Catherine Rodgers is lecturer in French at the University of Wales, Swansea.

Acknowledgements

The authors and publishers wish to thank the following for giving permission to reproduce extracts of the work of the prominent politicians and movements which illustrate each chapter.

Editions Stock for the passage from Jacques Chirac: *Discours pour la France à l'heure du choix* © Editions Stock, 1978.

Librairie Arthème Fayard for the passages from *Démocratie française* by Valéry Giscard d'Estaing © Librairie Arthème Fayard, 1976.

Editions Albatros for the passage from *Pour la France* by Jean-Marie Le Pen © Albatros, 1985.

Editions Nationales for the passages from *L'Alternative nationale, 300 mesures pour la renaissance de la France, Front national, Programme de gouvernement*, Paris: © Editions Nationales, 1993.

Librairie Arthème Fayard for the passages from *Ici et maintenant* by François Mitterrand © Librairie Arthème Fayard, 1980.

Editions du Seuil for the passage from *Un pays comme le nôtre* by Michel Rocard © Editions du Seuil, 1989.

Editions Messidor/Editions sociales for the passage from *Démocratie* by Georges Marchais © Messidor/Editions sociales, 1990.

Les Verts and *Génération Ecologie* for the reproduction of their *Accord programmatique* for the elections of 1993.

The CGT for reproducing documentation published subsequent to the 41st and 44th Congresses.

Part I:

The Fifth Republic and its Constitution

N. A. ADDINALL

Introduction to the constitution

1. The birth of the Fifth Republic

Until the Revolution of 1789, France had known only one form of
political regime: absolute monarchy, under which all powers, legislative, executive, and judiciary, were concentrated in the hands of the
king, and which reached its culminating point with the reign of Louis
XIV (1638–1715).

The end of an authoritarian regime is almost invariably followed
by a backlash, and thus it is that the eighteenth-century philosophers,
Jean-Jacques Rousseau with his *Contrat social* at their head, argue
that sovereignty lies with the people and that therefore all governmental authority is instituted by man and not by God; kings are not
kings by divine right but by the will of the people. In truth, these
arguments were not new, and from St Thomas Aquinas onwards are
rehearsed by such as Suarez and Bellarmin in the sixteenth century;
their refutation by absolute monarchists such as Bossuet led to the
absolute monarchy of Louis XIV, and the refutation of absolute
monarchy in the eighteenth century led to the Revolution of 1789,
the recognition of the sovereignty of the people and the proclamation
of the First Republic in 1792. The principle of the government of the
people by the people was therefore established, but what form should
it take and what institutions would be required? In other words, what
kind of constitution should the country have?

The answer to this question weighed heavily not only with the
Revolutionaries but also with their successors over the next eighty
odd years. During this period France experienced every kind of
constitution ranging from the First Republic to the Empire of
Napoleon, the relatively absolute monarchy of Louis XVIII and

Charles X, the constitutional monarchy of Louis-Philippe, the Second Republic of 1848, the Empire of Napoleon III and finally the Third Republic of 1870 after France's defeat in the Franco-Prussian War of 1870. Until the birth of the Third Republic the answers to political and social problems were believed to be found in modifying the ways in which the will of the people could be expressed – in short in changing the constitution.

With the Third Republic, this changed. Although the return of the monarchy remained a possibility until 1876,[1] it was broadly accepted thereafter and particularly after 1892 that the Republican form of government is the one most suited to France. Quarrels from that time on, or at least until the First World War, revolved around anticlericalism and the Third Republic's crusade against the Catholic church and its influence in all fields, but more particularly in that of education.[2]

As an answer to all political problems this crusade was hardly sufficient, but it did function quite well as a cementing agent to keep all Republicans united in face of the supposed threat of Catholicism.

The First World War and its aftermath helped to change all that. The truce in political warfare which had been declared in order to present a united front to German aggression, and the subsequent need to rebuild the country's economy after the war effort, meant that traditional political dividing lines concerning Church/State relationships had become somewhat outdated. In the years immediately following the First World War, economic concerns were not of primary concern as the French economy, unlike others, appeared to be basically sound. It is, no doubt, for this reason that the political impact of the Russian Revolution of 1917 was relatively slight in France, leading only to the short-lived period in power between 1924 and 1926 of the Cartel des Gauches, which was not inspired or led by Communists.

The thirties, however, saw major developments in the emergence of a new political force on the world stage, fascism, and the consolidation of its natural rival, communism, at the head of the ideologies ranged against it. At the same time, the Wall Street crash and the Depression led to the near ruin of the United States and other

---

[1] The monarchist majority elected in 1871 had high hopes of restoring the Comte de Chambord to the throne; the enmity between absolute and constitutional monarchists prevented this from happening.

[2] For an excellent description of what crusading Third Republic lay primary-school teachers were like, see M. Pagnol's *Souvenirs d'enfance*.

Western economies including, although later and in a less severe form, that of France itself. In the face of these economic problems and political choices France chose a left-wing solution and thus it was that the Front populaire government (comprising Socialist and Radical members with Communist support) was voted into power on 4 June 1936.

It was short-lived. The financial problems involved in trying to fund the wide-ranging social reforms (two weeks' paid annual leave, salary increases of between 7 and 15 per cent, reduction of the working week to forty hours, worker representation in business etc.), coupled with the vast increase in expenditure on defence in the face of the growing threat of the rise of fascism in Germany and in Spain (where civil war began in June 1936), as well as the ever-increasing number of strikes within the country, proved to be insoluble for Léon Blum's Front populaire government, which was forced to resign on 21 June 1937. Although Léon Blum was to reappear at the head of another government in March 1938, this and subsequent governments until the outbreak of war in 1939 were coalition governments, largely dominated by the Radical party. The Radical members' political credo is perhaps best summed up in the expression of the historian Siegfried, who said that they had 'their hearts on their left but their wallets on the right'.

Of more importance than their economic policies, however, was the fact that they were basically pacifists and it is not surprising therefore that the Radical head of a government composed almost entirely of Radical deputies, Edouard Daladier, should have been the co-signatory with Chamberlain on 29 September 1938 of the Munich agreement, which surrendered Czechoslovakia to the mercies of Hitler.

The Radicals were not alone, however, in their pacificism. The French Socialist party (known as the SFIO under the Third and Fourth Republics) also had a long tradition of pacifism going back to Jean Jaurès and his preaching that the working class is the principal victim of warfare, as was demonstrated, after his assassination, by the holocaust of the First World War. It is true, as mentioned above, that Blum's Front populaire governments spent quite heavily on defence, but not nearly enough or soon enough for the Communists who had firmly perceived the danger posed by fascism at a much earlier stage. That the money was being spent on antiquated methods of warfare instead of on tanks and planes was also pointed out by one of the foremost theoreticians of modern warfare who had

already published works on the subject. His name was Colonel
Charles de Gaulle.

The scope of this book does not allow for a detailed examination
of the Second World War. Suffice it to say that after the invasion of
France by Germany in May 1940, the signing of an armistice by
Marshal Pétain and the creation under his command of a so-called
French State based at Vichy, the rest of France being under German
occupation, the war effort against the Germans was continued outside
France by Charles de Gaulle, by that time a general, with his launch-
ing of the Free French movement (*Forces françaises libres*) on 18
June 1940 and, within France, by the Resistance movement.

As a result of the heroics of the Free French and the Resistance,
the political scene in France at the end of the war in 1945 was dominated by General de Gaulle on the one hand, and the political parties
– foremost amongst them the Communist party – which had provided
the backbone of the Resistance on the other.

On one thing all were agreed: the Third Republic had disappeared
never to return when Pétain signed the armistice with the Germans
on 22 June 1940. The defeat of France had been due to the creak-
ing inefficiency of an elderly and worn-out Republic which now
needed replacement as a matter of urgency. Much faith and hope
was therefore placed in a new Fourth Republic which would correspond to the aspirations of those who had fought so hard with the
Allies to liberate France.

On the form it should take, however, the victors were divided. For
General de Gaulle, the lesson was absolutely clear. The Third Republic had failed because the multiplicity of political parties in the
Chamber of Deputies, and the continued warfare between them, had
meant that every government had been a makeshift coalition, unable
to carry out any coherent policies before being voted out. The executive power had therefore been extremely weak, and this was
compounded by the very limited role of the president of the Republic. For de Gaulle, therefore, the powers of the government and of
the president of the Republic needed to be increased, and those of
the elected assembly (*Assemblée nationale*) reduced.

The view of the majority of the political parties, particularly the
Communists, was very different, and it is not difficult to understand
why. Apart from the fact that it was obviously in their own interests
that the elected assembly should be all-powerful as that was where
they were represented and where the legislative power lay, there were
the further considerations, in their view, that democracy means that

maximum power should be given to the representatives of the people in order to execute the will of the people, and that the dark forces of fascism having been defeated a new era was now dawning which would allow, just like during the Revolution, the flowering of new ideas and the creation of a new, dynamic and democratic society.

The conflict between these opposing views led to the Constituent Assembly coming up with a proposal for a constitution to be put to the people by referendum, corresponding in particular to the views of the left-wing parties. It proposed the creation of a single elected Assembly which would elect the president of the Republic, the prime minister and the ministers and which would wield, *ipso facto*, the executive power as well as the legislative power. The result of the referendum held on 5 May 1946 is not therefore particularly surprising: 47 per cent voted in favour of the proposal, but 53 per cent voted against.

A less extreme version of the same constitution was therefore prepared for a new referendum which was held on 13 October and this time approximately 9 million votes were cast in favour and approximately 8 million against, there being some 6 million abstentions.

Although modified, the new constitution of the Fourth Republic was none the less in much the same spirit as the previous model. Although it created two Chambers, an *Assemblée nationale* and a *Conseil de la République*, the latter had very few powers and it was the former, the home of the political parties, which wielded not only the legislative power but virtually all the executive power as well since it elected the prime minister and also, together with the *Conseil de la République*, the president of the Republic. To try to give some stability to the government, the constitution gave the government the right to dissolve the *Assemblée nationale* if it was voted out, but this measure was insufficient to give stability to a regime which, in its twelve years of existence, was to have no fewer than twenty-five governments.

Was this instability due only to what General de Gaulle called the 'jeu de partis'? In part yes, but one also has to look at the immense problems and difficulties with which the Fourth Republic was faced during its brief existence. Not only did it have to rebuild the country after the destruction caused by the war but, more importantly, it found itself immediately and successively involved in colonial wars in Indo-China and Algeria, the latter of which was to bring its days to an end in something considerably less than the euphoria with which the left-wing parties in particular had greeted its birth.

The war in Indo-China (1946–54), fought to recover French possessions at the end of the war, was a bloody and protracted struggle, but the fact that the all-important battle of Dien Bien Phu was lost against the well-armed Viet-Minh and that there was no large-scale, long-term population of French settlers installed there to complicate matters made the task of M. Mendès-France and his government, when they brought the war to an end in 1954, somewhat simpler than that faced by successive governments with the war in Algeria.

Algeria was in many ways a different problem from Indo-China. It had a large French population of over 1 million, some of whom had come after the conquest of the country in 1830, but most of them had come after the Franco-Prussian war of 1870. Many of these were not rich settlers but 'poor whites' who had never seen France and for whom Algeria was their home. There was a further complication in that many of those, including army officers, who were ferociously in favour of Algeria remaining French, were so because they believed that Algeria should become an integral part of France and that Algerians should become French citizens; for such proponents of this solution as the former minister of General de Gaulle, Jacques Soustelle, the choice was not between independence for Algeria or remaining a French colony, but between independence for Algeria or becoming an important region of France. This dilemma was exacerbated by the fact that by 1957 the French army appeared to have won the war against the Algerian *Front de libération nationale* (FLN); it is easy to see why successive governments found it impossible simply to sign a peace agreement with the FLN and withdraw from the country.

At the same time it was no easier simply to declare Algeria part of France. In spite of military successes, it was fairly obvious that a force such as the FLN could not be held permanently in check without vast expenditure on a huge occupying force, and it was also clear that the integration of Algeria into France would entail the spending of further vast sums on the provision of social protection, benefits and services for its citizens henceforth entitled to the same advantages as French nationals. Huge spending would also be required on communications, infra-structure and so on.

In short, succeeding French governments under the Socialist Guy Mollet (31 January 1956–21 May 1957), the Radical Bourgès-Maunoury (13 June 1957–30 September 1957), the Radical Félix Gaillard (6 November 1957–15 April 1958) and finally Pierre Pflimlin, the leading member of the MRP (*Mouvement républicain populaire*, the centre right party) attempted without success to bring the war to an end.

It was, in fact, on the very day that the last-named was appointed prime minister, on 13 May 1958, that an uprising in favour of *Algérie française* took place in Algiers and a *Comité de Salut public* was set up with the famous paratrooper General Massu at its head. The fear now was that the army would not only take over completely in Algeria but would send the paratroops to take Paris by storm and impose a military dictatorship.

How could this, and consequential civil war, be prevented? By 15 May it had been made clear by General Massu and the commander-in-chief, General Salan, that the return to power of General de Gaulle would be an acceptable solution for them as they thought that he shared their belief in *Algérie française*, and on the same day General de Gaulle let it be known that he held himself ready to 'assumer les pouvoirs de la République'.

But could this be an acceptable solution for the political parties? Would it not be inviting General de Gaulle to return as a dictator? The question was put to him at a press conference on 19 May and his reply is well known: 'Pourquoi voulez-vous qu'à 67 ans je commence une carrière de dictateur!'

The parties did not have a great deal of choice in the matter, however. They certainly knew that the taking of Paris by the paratroops was planned for 28 May and thus negotiations enabled General de Gaulle to declare on 27 May that: 'J'ai entamé hier le processus régulier nécessaire à l'établissement d'un pouvoir républicain capable d'assurer l'unité et l'indépendance du pays.' The planned military coup was thus called off, and on 29 May the president of the Republic, René Coty, announced to the *Assemblée nationale* that he intended appointing General de Gaulle, 'le plus illustre des Français', as prime minister. The latter accepted on condition that this be a prelude to putting a proposal before the people for a new constitution, to be voted on by referendum. On 1 June he was sworn in, and on 3 June the Assembly voted to give him emergency powers which included the right to revise the constitution. Immediately afterwards he set off to Algiers to utter his famous 'Je vous ai compris', leading Salan, Massu and the others to believe he was with them, whilst managing not to declare openly that he was in favour of 'Algérie française'. In fact he was personally opposed to it and wished to see an independent Algeria for reasons which are detailed in his *Mémoires* but which are largely to do with freedom, economics and national identity. It was, however, to take this extra-ordinary man another four years, and an ability to survive several assassination attempts, before he was able to bring the Algerian war to an end.

The end of the Fourth Republic, on the other hand, was immediate, and the constitution of the new Fifth Republic was put to the people on 28 September 1958. The result of the referendum was a massive majority in favour: 17,668,790 in favour, 4,624,511 against, and 4,016,614 abstentions.

2. The constitution of the Fifth Republic

It will be clear from preceding remarks that General de Gaulle's new constitution would bear little resemblance to the previous one. Whereas under the Fourth Republic the political parties had sought, for reasons seen, to make the elected assembly – the *Assemblée nationale* – supreme, effectively giving it executive powers as well as legislative powers, General de Gaulle sought in the constitution of the Fifth Republic to reduce the powers of the elected assembly and increase those of both the government and the president of the Republic, to enable the government to govern, and the president of the Republic to be more than just a figure-head.

The order of the different titles indicates this clearly. Whereas the Fourth Republic had put *le Parlement* (*Assemblée nationale* and *Conseil de la République*) first, followed by the *Conseil économique*, then the president of the Republic, and firmly in last place, the government, the constitution of the Fifth Republic almost reverses the order, putting the president of the Republic first, the government second and *le Parlement* third.

What was the rationale behind putting the president of the Republic first, and what powers does the constitution give this office? The rationale is not hard to understand, given the character and experiences of General de Gaulle. Apart from a natural instinct to consider the presence of a paternal figure as being not only desirable but necessary, in order to act as an arbiter if conflicts should occur between the legislative and executive powers, there was the further salutary lesson provided by the last war as to what could happen to a state when its legislative and executive powers can no longer function due to invasion. General de Gaulle argued that if in 1940 there had been a president of the Republic endowed with constitutional powers making him a real head of state instead of just a figure-head, it would have been altogether easier for such a person to have gathered all the elements of resistance to the Germans around him and to have continued the war against them, instead of leaving the job to someone, not exactly the 'premier venu', but none the less a *général de brigade* who was little known, even within France itself.

These twin preoccupations are reflected in the powers which the constitution confers on the president of the Republic and the essential elements of which are set out in the extracts from the constitution reproduced below.

The first preoccupation is illustrated clearly by Article 5 of the constitution; the job of the president is to make sure that the constitution is respected and that the political game is played according to the rules. As the referee, he can theoretically sanction either side (the government or the *Assemblée nationale*) if they try to infringe on the rules. These sanctions are incorporated in Articles 8 and 12. The second preoccupation is also illustrated here; the president is in the final analysis responsible for making sure that the country's independence and borders are defended to the last – this aspect will be developed in Article 16.

If he is to fulfil this role of being an independent, impartial and respected arbiter, it follows that he must be more than just the representative of a political party: he must look to protect the general and national interest, and not that of a particular section of society as represented by the different political parties. This, in turn, means that presidential elections should not be held at the same time as general elections (*élections législatives*) as the likelihood would be that the electorate would vote for a presidential candidate of the same hue as the majority political party(ies) elected, in which case the president would not be an independent figure but a representative of his party, and thereby a single party would control the *Assemblée nationale* (through its majority), the government (since the government must perforce be chosen from the party(ies) having the majority in the *Assemblée nationale*, otherwise it would be voted out of office) and the presidency of the Republic. In brief, this would place all three powers in the hands of one political party, which was not exactly what General de Gaulle and his advisers had in mind, although, as will be discussed below, the constitution has indeed functioned in this way, and particularly under General de Gaulle.

In order to underline the difference between the functions of the legislative and the executive powers and those of the president of the

Republic, it was decided, therefore, that whereas *députés* (members of Parliament) in the *Assemblée nationale* should be elected for a period of five years, the president should be elected for seven years (Article 6).

If the president of the Republic is to represent the general and national interest it is also essential that the votes cast for him or her, under a system of universal suffrage, should amount to more than 50 per cent. There can be no question of a 'first-past-the-post' system whereby a candidate, having secured less than half of the vote of the total population, can pretend to speak in the name of the population as a whole. This is why the two-round presidential electoral system exists under the Fifth Republic (see Article 7 below) or has done so since the modification of the constitution of 6 November 1962 – prior to this the president was elected for seven years by an electoral college comprising members of Parliament, members of *conseils généraux*, *conseils municipaux* and overseas-territories assemblies. If no candidate obtains an absolute majority in the first round – which is normally the case given the number of candidates – the two candidates who have gained the greatest number of votes meet in a second round, which decides who is the winner.

The following Articles 8, 9 and 10, plus Articles 12 and 13, give the president of the Republic powers which again correspond to those of the arbiter.

Article 8 states that the president appoints the prime minister and accepts his or her resignation, but does this mean that the president can appoint the person he or she prefers, and dismiss that person when liked? Or is it not the case that the president has to appoint somebody approved by a majority? And in what circumstances can the president accept the prime minister's resignation?

Article 9 states that the president of the Republic presides over Cabinet meetings, but this does not mean that that role as chairperson gives the president the right to tell the government what to do.

Article 10 indicates that the president of the Republic has officially to promulgate laws which have been passed, but that he or she has a fortnight during which it is possible to demand that a law or some of its articles be re-presented before the *Assemblée nationale*. This does not allow the president to modify legislation. Does it give him or her more powers, however, than those of an arbiter?

Article 12 allows the president of the Republic to dissolve the *Assemblée nationale*. But this does not enable the president to hold new elections in order to change its composition whenever he or she likes, for the simple practical reason that a president would only do so when he or she is certain of his or her own party winning a majority.

Article 13 states that the president of the Republic signs the edicts and decrees decided on in Cabinet. If he or she refuses to do so, he or she can oblige the government to have the subject of each one voted on by the *Assemblée nationale*, but as the government always has a majority in the *Assemblée nationale*, this can never be more than a delaying tactic.

These articles have been interpreted in different ways, and may be thought to give more power than that of an arbiter to the president of the Republic, but most controversy concerning quasi-dictatorial powers has arisen over Articles 11, 15 and 16.

Article 11 states that the president may consult the people by referendum, and whilst this is certainly a means for the president to bypass the *Assemblée nationale* and apparently act directly with the approval of the citizens, it is essential to note that the conditions under which the president can have recourse to a referendum are very closely defined (see article below). The president can only hold a referendum on matters affecting 'les pouvoirs publics' – in other words a modification to the constitution.

Article 15 states that the president of the Republic is 'le chef des armées' at the same time as Articles 20 and 21, under Title III *Le Gouvernement*, state that the government '. . . dispose de l'Administration et de la force armée' (Art. 20) and 'Il [le Premier ministre] est responsable de la Défense nationale' (Art. 21). There was much speculation during the first period of 'cohabitation' in 1986–8 (a left-wing president was in office at the same time as a right-wing majority in the *Assemblée nationale*, and therefore a right-wing government, this happening as a result of, as noted above, presidential elections being held every seven years, and general elections, *élections législatives*, every five years) as to whether the constitution made the president of the Republic or the prime minister the head of the armed forces. As it happened, the president (François Mitterrand) and the prime minister (Jacques Chirac) did not basically disagree on defence policy and this was not, therefore, a problem. The question is, however, to know whether this article gives more power to the president than that of an arbiter. Its very ambiguity undoubtedly supplies the answer; in time of peace, when there is no threat of invasion and the institutions can function normally, defence policy is just one of the issues which president and government can discuss together, but which the government, as the executive power, decides upon. In case of invasion of the country, however, and bearing in mind General de Gaulle's preoccupation with making the president of the Republic more than just a figure-head, there must be a head of state empowered by the constitution to place himself or herself at the head of the armed forces and continue the battle against the invader if the legislative and executive powers have been prevented, by the invasion, from carrying out their functions in a normal manner. In short, it does not, in normal circumstances, give the president of the Republic greater powers over the armed forces than those of the prime minister and his or her government.

Article 16 is the article which caused most controversy as it was considered by some commentators to give the president of the Republic dictatorial powers at moments of his own choosing, thereby going far beyond the role of arbiter. The article is reproduced below and the reader will see that it does indeed give the president full powers to take the measures 'exigées par ces circonstances' when 'les institutions de la République, l'indépendance de la nation, l'intégrité de son territoire ou l'exécution de ses engagements internationaux sont menacées d'une manière grave et immédiate . . .' It has been argued that the president himself or herself can define when 'institutions', 'indépendance', 'intégrité', etc. are threatened and thereby afford himself or herself full powers at moments of his or her own choosing. Even if the article also says that the president must consult the prime minister, the presidents of the Assemblies and the *Conseil constitutionnel*, it does not, it has been argued, mean that he or she has to listen to the advice received!

Such criticisms, however, neglect the fact that this article also says that the president of the Republic can only take on full powers when 'le fonctionnement régulier des pouvoirs publics constitutionnels est interrompu' – in other words when the *Assemblée nationale*, the *Sénat*, and the government, the legislative and executive powers, are unable to function normally. This can only happen in case of invasion or civil war and it is clear that General de Gaulle's intention here was not to give dictatorial powers to the president of the Republic but to give that office the constitutional means to continue the fight against the enemy in case of invasion.

It will be seen from the preceding comments that the president of the Republic has certain powers that enable him or her to have a certain importance in the choice of government, in the timing of elections through his or her power to dissolve the *Assemblée nationale*, in consulting the people by referendum on matters pertaining to a modification to the constitution, and in chairmanship of meetings of the Cabinet. It is clear, however, that these are passive powers which do not allow the president to take the initiative in either the legislative or executive fields. As we have also seen, those articles which appear to give the president far greater powers are only operable in extreme conditions such as invasion of the country.

If all this is true, then why should the powers of the president of the Republic, as pointed out earlier, appear as the first title in the constitution, and why should different presidents of the Republic, particularly Charles de Gaulle, have acted as if they enjoyed far greater powers than these?

The answer to the first question is that de Gaulle certainly wished to increase the powers of the president in order to give the holder of that office the constitutional power to act as an arbiter between the legislative and executive powers in normal circumstances and as the leader of the country in extreme circumstances such as the invasion of France in 1940, but he was also perfectly aware that to afford the president powers greater than these would be to make out a blueprint for a dictatorship; even if the presidency has a passive participating role, it must never be in charge of the legislative or executive powers.

This brings us to the second question, and it has to be said that all presidents of the Republic and particularly Charles de Gaulle, have changed prime ministers as they thought fit, and often acted as if they were at the head of both the legislative and executive powers. The reasons for this do not lie in the constitution, however. They lie in the fact that the president of the Republic has so far always been not only a member of a political party, but also the head of it.

De Gaulle provides the most striking example of this. Brought to power in 1958 in the conditions described above, he had at his disposal a party which existed only by and for himself, the *Union pour la Nouvelle République* (UNR). Accordingly, he could decide, as his own party had an enormous majority, who the prime minister should be, and could change him as he thought fit. Thus it was that de Gaulle changed prime ministers on his own initiative, appointing successively Michel Debré (8 January 1959–14 April 1962), Georges Pompidou (14 April 1962–21 July 1968) and Maurice Couve de Murville (21 July 1968–16 June 1969).

This pattern was continued by Georges Pompidou (president 1969–74), who appointed Jacques Chaban-Delmas as prime minister on 20 June 1969 and replaced him by Pierre Messmer on 7 July 1972. After the short 'Regency' of Alain Poher (2 April–19 May

1974) (for the second time, having already been a provisional president of the Republic after de Gaulle's resignation between 28 April and 19 June 1969), the new president, Valéry Giscard d'Estaing was elected on 19 May 1974. He, in turn, appointed first Jacques Chirac, on 28 May 1974, and then Raymond Barre on 27 August 1976. François Mitterrand was Giscard's successor as president of the Republic, elected on 21 May 1981, and he also changed prime ministers, appointing successively Pierre Mauroy (21 May 1981), Laurent Fabius (19 July 1984), Jacques Chirac (20 June 1986), Michel Rocard (12 May 1988), Edith Cresson (15 May 1991, the first female prime minister) and Pierre Bérégovoy (2 April 1992). After the heavy defeat at the general election of 1993, Mitterrand was obliged, as in 1986 with Chirac, to appoint a prime minister from the ranks of the right-wing majority in the *Assemblée nationale*. 'Cohabitation' (the co-existence of a president of the Republic of one political hue and a majority in the *Assemblée nationale*, and therefore a government, of another) thus returned, but the prime minister this time was not Chirac, but Balladur, a prominent member of Chirac's party, the RPR, who proved so popular with the French electorate that he dared to stand against Chirac in the presidential elections of April and May 1995. His hopes were dashed when he was beaten into third place in the first ballot by Chirac and the Socialist candidate Jospin. Chirac was the victor in the second round play-off and, not surprisingly, he decided to dispense with Balladur's services as prime minister, replacing him with Juppé.

It will be seen from the above that the constitution of the Fifth Republic gives only passive powers to the president of the Republic in normal circumstances, the active role that some presidents have enjoyed being due to the fact that they were at the head of political parties having a majority in the *Assemblée nationale*.

This presidential function is unique to the Fifth Republic. The United States also has a presidential system, but the president there replaces the prime minister as the head of the executive power. Other countries, such as the United Kingdom, have a head of state or monarch, but who acts only as a figure-head, the executive power being in the hands of the prime minister.

The government

General de Gaulle believed firmly in reinforcing the executive power and giving the government the means to govern. Whereas he believed that the powers of the president of the Republic should also be strengthened, it will be clear from the above examination that the constitution does not confer on the president the powers of the executive body, which are, quite properly, those of the government.

Articles 20 and 21 of the Constitution, as illustrated below, make this crystal clear. Article 20 states that the government 'détermine et conduit la politique de la Nation' and Article 21 states that 'le Premier ministre dirige l'action du Gouvernement.'

This said, it is important to note that, as in any parliamentary democracy, the government is answerable to the citizens' representatives in the elected Assembly for its actions and this is why Article 49 (see below) states that 'L'Assemblée nationale met en cause la responsabilité de Gouvernement par le vote d'une motion de censure.' This article also states that the government can request a vote of confidence in its policies before the *Assemblée nationale*.

These safeguards would appear to indicate that the government is powerless unless it has the full support of the majority in the *Assemblée nationale*, and whilst this is largely true it is none the less the case that the constitution outlines areas which pertain particularly to the legislative power on the one hand or the executive power on the other. Article 34 (see below) defines the areas in which the legislative power is competent, and Article 37 (see below) states categorically that all other matters 'ont un caractère réglementaire', which means they are decided by the government, which can impose measures by decrees and edicts. Furthermore, Article 38 (see below) empowers the government to ask the *Assemblée nationale* for permission to govern by decree in matters which normally pertain to the legislative power, as outlined in Article 34. As the government is always chosen from the ranks of the majority in the elected *Assemblée nationale*, this means that the government can effectively govern by decree. The only exception to this is when the president of the Republic is not of the same political persuasion as the government, in which case he or she can refuse to sign the decrees (Article 13, see below), thus obliging the government to have recourse to the normal procedure of putting its 'projets de loi' before the *Assemblée nationale*. This can be no more than a delaying tactic, however, on the part of the president of the Republic, as it is obvious that the government's majority in the *Assemblée nationale* will vote in the way that the government wishes it to vote.

The *Parlement*

The *Parlement* is composed of two assemblies, the *Assemblée nationale* and the *Sénat*.

The *députés* in the *Assemblée nationale* (members of parliament) are elected by direct universal suffrage for a period of five years and the *sénateurs* are elected by an electoral college composed of *députés, conseillers généraux* (see below) and some *conseillers municipaux* (town councillors, see below) for a period of nine years. Elections are held every three years, however, as a third of the Senate is renewed every three years.

Article 28 states that the *Parlement* meets normally for two sessions per year. The first begins on 2 October and lasts for eighty days, the second begins on 2 April and lasts for a maximum of ninety days, unless these dates coincide with a bank holiday in which case the sessions begin on the first following working day. Article 29 adds that *Parlement* may be recalled at the behest of the prime minister or the majority of the members of the *Assemblée nationale* to discuss a particular agenda.

The president of the *Assemblée nationale* is elected for five years' duration between elections, and the president of the *Sénat* is elected after each three-year partial renewal of *sénateurs*.

The powers of the *Parlement* are as defined in Article 34 below, but basically enable it to vote on bills put before it by the government or individual *députés* or *sénateurs*, to vote on the Budget, to put written or oral questions to the government and – in the case of the *Assemblée nationale*, but not the *Sénat* – to bring down the government by voting a 'motion de censure' or refusing to back it on a vote of 'confiance' (Article 49).

3. Modifications to the constitution

Apart from the modification of 6 November 1962 providing for the election of the president of the Republic by universal suffrage, there have been few major changes made to the constitution of the Fifth Republic. A major change that has often been suggested, however, and most significantly, by succeeding presidents of the Republic, Pompidou, Giscard d'Estaing and Mitterrand, is to reduce the term of office of the president from seven years to five years, in order to make it correspond to the length of term of the *Assemblée nationale* and thereby avoid the situation which has twice arisen (from 1986 to 1988 and 1993 to 1995) in which the president of the Republic holds different political views from those of the majority in the *Assemblée nationale*, and therefore the government. This modification has yet to be put to the nation, however, and President Chirac, whilst not being completely opposed, has not expressed a desire to hold a referendum on the matter in the near future.

Mitterrand did, in fact, appoint a *Comité consultatif* in November 1992 whose task was to look at different propositions for reforming the constitution in order to, amongst other things, 'assurer un meilleur équilibre des pouvoirs'. The committee came up with a number of suggestions, but reducing the term of the presidency was not one of these, and of the others the government of Balladur decided to retain only very minor reforms concerning the *Haute Cour de justice* and the *Conseil supérieur de la magistrature*.

If the presidential term is reduced from seven years to five, it is clear that presidential and parliamentary/governmental terms will normally coincide, which means that president and government will normally belong to the same political party and thereby presidential, legislative and executive powers will be united. This certainly makes for efficiency in government, but does it not change the concept of the president of the Republic as an impartial, paternal head of state representing the people as a whole, and remaining aloof from the partisan political struggle? The two periods of cohabitation have shown that there are advantages in having a president of the Republic who can disagree with the government and thereby act as a moderating influence on what may be viewed as some of its excesses.

4. Other representative bodies

The scope of this book does not allow for discussion of the French legal system or of a detailed examination of the *Conseil constitutionnel* and the *Conseil économique et social*. Suffice it to say that the *Conseil constitutionnel* checks the regularity of electoral procedures and is broadly responsible for making sure that the constitution is respected, whilst the *Conseil économique et social* advises the government on matters pertaining to the economic and social life of the country.

Important as these bodies may be, they do not represent the political will of the nation, which is expressed not only through the

Assemblée nationale and the *Sénat* but also through regional and local councils known as the *Conseil régional*, the *Conseil général de département* and the *Conseil municipal*.

Conseils régionaux

Part of the Socialist government's drive to reduce central government power and increase decentralization, these were created by the law on decentralization of 2 March 1982 which transferred to the regions powers which had hitherto been the prerogative of the State.

The *régions* are made up of two or more *départements* which have economic interests and geographical boundaries in common. There are twenty-two *régions* in mainland France, plus the four overseas territories of Guadeloupe, Guyane, Martinique and Ile de la Réunion.

The regional councillors are elected for six years by direct universal suffrage and are responsible, with the State, for planning and executing the economic and social development of the region. This means expenditure on roads, railways, ports, education, housing, town and country planning, cultural activities and so on.

Financing comes directly from the State, borrowing, local taxes and taxes on driving licences and vehicle registration documents.

The *président* (chairperson) is elected by the regional councillors.

Conseils généraux de département

Like the *Conseils régionaux*, these were created, in their present form, by the law on decentralization of 2 March 1982 and have responsibility for planning the economic and social development of the smaller unit which is the *département*. There are ninety-six *départements* in mainland France and five overseas *départements*, which are composed of the above-mentioned *régions* of Guadeloupe, Guyane, Martinique and Ile de la Réunion, plus St Pierre et Miquelon.

The *conseillers généraux* are elected for six years by direct universal suffrage and are responsible, with the aid of the State, for expenditure on welfare benefits, allowances, medical prevention measures such as vaccination, social services, departmental roads, infrastructure and buildings (libraries, *gendarmeries*, etc.) as well as the building and maintenance of secondary schools and the general provision of services to those living in rural environments. The *président* (chairperson) is elected by the *conseillers généraux*.

As is the case for the *Conseils régionaux*, financing comes from the State but also from local taxes on property and others such as the *vignette* (road tax). Before the law on decentralization of 2 March 1982 the powers of the *Conseil général* were mainly in the hands of government representatives known since the Revolution as *préfets* and *sous-préfets*. This law changed their name to *commissaires de la République*, but a further law of 24 February 1988 restored their title although not their powers.

Conseils municipaux

These are town or village councils, representing the *commune*, which can vary enormously in size from less than 100 inhabitants to more than 300,000. The councillors are elected for six years by direct universal suffrage, and their number varies, according to the size of the population, from nine to well over a hundred. The mayor is elected, from amongst their number, by the councillors.

The duties of the town or village council vary, depending on its size, but normally include basic services such as upkeep of roads, building and maintenance of primary schools, kindergarten, sports grounds and leisure centres, as well as the provision of refuse disposal collections, a police force and the organizing of cultural and sporting activities of all kinds, such as exhibitions, concerts, and the reception of visiting touring teams.

The mayor is also the representative, on the local plane, of the Republic, and as such enjoys certain responsibilities entrusted to him by the State. These include bringing to public awareness laws and decrees and organizing elections, but his most prominent public role is almost certainly when he officiates as the representative of the French Republic at civil marriage ceremonies.

5. Electoral systems

It is to be noted that whereas voting in the presidential, legislative and *Conseil général de département* elections is for individual candidates (*scrutin uninominal*) by direct universal suffrage, candidates for the *Conseils municipaux*, *Conseils régionaux* and European Parliament elections stand for election in party lists and seats are attributed according to a system of proportional representation (*scrutin de liste à représentation proportionnelle*).

As indicated above, *sénateurs* are elected by indirect universal suffrage. Departments having up to four *sénateurs* use the two-round majority party list system (*scrutin de liste majoritaire à deux tours*) and those entitled to more than four *sénateurs* use a system of party lists with proportional representation (*scrutin de liste à représentation proportionnelle*).

Sources

Key articles from the constitution

1. Concerning the president of the Republic

Article 5

Le Président de la République veille au respect de la Constitution. Il assure, par son arbitrage, le fonctionnement régulier des pouvoirs publics ainsi que la continuité de l'Etat.

Il est le garant de l'indépendance nationale, de l'intégrité du territoire, du respect des accords de Communauté et des traités.

Article 6

(*L. n° 62-1292 du 6 novembre 1962*) Le Président de la République est élu pour sept ans au suffrage universel direct.

Les modalités d'application du présent article sont fixées par une loi organique.

Article 7

(*L. n° 62-1292 du 6 novembre 1962*) Le Président de la République est élu à la majorité absolue des suffrages exprimés. Si celle-ci n'est pas obtenue au premier tour de scrutin, il est procédé, le deuxième dimanche suivant, à un second tour. Seuls peuvent s'y présenter les deux candidats qui, le cas échéant après retrait de candidats plus favorisés, se trouvent avoir recueilli le plus grand nombre de suffrages au premier tour.

Le scrutin est ouvert sur convocation du Gouvernement.

L'élection du nouveau Président a lieu vingt jours au moins et trente-cinq jours au plus avant l'expiration des pouvoirs du Président en exercice.

En cas de vacance de la présidence de la République pour quelque cause que ce soit, ou d'empêchement constaté par le Conseil constitutionnel saisi par le Gouvernement et statuant à la majorité absolue de ses membres, les fonctions du Président de la

République, à l'exception de celles prévues aux articles 11 et 12 ci-dessous, sont provisoirement exercées par le président du Sénat et, si celui-ci est à son tour empêché d'exercer ces fonctions, par le Gouvernement.

En cas de vacance ou lorsque l'empêchement est déclaré définitif par le Conseil constitutionnel, le scrutin pour l'élection du nouveau Président a lieu, sauf cas de force majeure constaté par le Conseil constitutionnel, vingt jours au moins et trente-cinq jours au plus après l'ouverture de la vacance ou la déclaration du caractère définitif de l'empêchement.

(*L. const. n° 76-527 du 18 juin 1976*). Si, dans les sept jours précédant la date limite du dépôt des présentations de candidatures, une des personnes ayant, moins de trente jours avant cette date, annoncé publiquement sa décision d'être candidate décède ou se trouve empêchée, le Conseil constitutionnel peut décider de reporter l'élection.

Si, avant le premier tour, un des candidats décède ou se trouve empêché, le Conseil constitutionnel prononce le report de l'élection.

En cas de décès ou d'empêchement de l'un des deux candidats les plus favorisés au premier tour avant les retraits éventuels, le Conseil constitutionnel déclare qu'il doit être procédé de nouveau à l'ensemble des opérations électorales; il en est de même en cas de décès ou d'empêchement de l'un des deux candidats restés en présence en vue du second tour.

Dans tous les cas, le Conseil constitutionnel est saisi dans les conditions fixées au deuxième alinéa de l'article 61 ci-dessous ou dans celles déterminées pour la présentation d'un candidat par la loi organique prévue à l'article 6 ci-dessus.

Le Conseil constitutionnel peut proroger les délais prévus aux troisième et cinquième alinéas sans que le scrutin puisse avoir lieu plus de trente-cinq jours après la date de la décision du Conseil constitutionnel. Si l'application des dispositions du présent alinéa a eu pour effet de reporter l'élection à une date postérieure à l'expiration des pouvoirs du Président en exercice, celui-ci demeure en fonction jusqu'à la proclamation de son successeur.

(*L. N° 62-1292 du 6 novembre 1962*) Il ne peut être fait application ni des articles 49 et 50 ni de l'article 89 de la Constitution durant la vacance de la présidence de la République ou durant la période qui s'écoule entre la déclaration du caractère définitif de l'empêchement du Président de la République et l'élection de son successeur.

Article 8

Le Président de la République nomme le Premier ministre. Il met fin à ses fonctions sur la présentation par celui-ci de la démission du Gouvernement.

Sur la proposition du Premier ministre, il nomme les autres membres du Gouvernement et met fin à leurs fonctions.

Article 9

Le Président de la République préside le Conseil des ministres.

Article 10

Le Président de la République promulgue les lois dans les quinze jours qui suivent la transmission au Gouvernement de la loi définitivement adoptée.

Il peut, avant l'expiration de ce délai, demander au Parlement une nouvelle délibération de la loi ou de certains de ses articles. Cette nouvelle délibération ne peut être refusée.

Article 11

Le Président de la République, sur proposition du Gouvernement pendant la durée des sessions ou sur proposition conjointe des deux assemblées, publiée au *Journal officiel*, peut soumettre au référendum tout projet de loi portant sur l'organisation des pouvoirs publics, comportant approbation d'un accord de Communauté ou tendant à autoriser la ratification d'un traité qui, sans être contraire à la Constitution, aurait des incidences sur le fonctionnement des institutions.

Lorsque le référendum a conclu à l'adoption du projet, le Président de la République le promulgue dans le délai prévu à l'article précédent.

Article 12

Le Président de la République peut, après consultation du Premier ministre et des présidents des assemblées, prononcer la dissolution de l'Assemblée nationale.

Les élections générales ont lieu vingt jours au moins et quarante jours au plus après la dissolution.

L'Assemblée nationale se réunit de plein droit le deuxième jeudi qui suit son élection. Si cette réunion a lieu en dehors des périodes prévues pour les sessions ordinaires, une session est ouverte de droit pour une durée de quinze jours.

Il ne peut être procédé à une nouvelle dissolution dans l'année qui suit ces élections.

Article 13

Le Président de la République signe les ordonnances et les décrets délibérés en Conseil des ministres.

Il nomme aux emplois civils et militaires.

Les conseillers d'Etat, le grand chancelier de la Légion d'honneur, les ambassadeurs et envoyés extraordinaires, les conseillers maîtres à la Cour des comptes, les préfets, les représentants du Gouvernement dans les territoires d'outre-mer, les officiers généraux, les recteurs des académies, les directeurs des administrations centrales sont nommés en Conseil des ministres.

Une loi organique détermine les autres emplois auxquels il est pourvu en Conseil des ministres ainsi que les conditions dans lesquelles le pouvoir de nomination du Président de la République peut être par lui délégué pour être exercé en son nom.

Article 15

Le Président de la République est le chef des armées. Il préside les conseils et comités supérieurs de la Défense nationale.

Article 16

Lorsque les institutions de la République, l'indépendance de la nation, l'intégrité de son territoire ou l'exécution de ses engagements internationaux sont menacés d'une manière grave et immédiate et que le fonctionnement régulier des pouvoirs publics constitutionnels est interrompu, le Président de la République prend les mesures exigées par ces circonstances, après consultation officielle du Premier ministre, des présidents des assemblées ainsi que du Conseil constitutionnel.

Il en informe la nation par un message.

Ces mesures doivent être inspirées par la volonté d'assurer aux pouvoirs publics constitutionnels, dans les moindres délais, les moyens d'accomplir leur mission. Le Conseil constitutionnel est consulté à leur sujet.

Le Parlement se réunit de plein droit.

L'Assemblée nationale ne peut être dissoute pendant l'exercice des pouvoirs exceptionnels.

2. Concerning the Government

Article 20

Le Gouvernement détermine et conduit la politique de la Nation.

Il dispose de l'Administration et de la force armée.

Il est responsable devant le Parlement dans les conditions et suivant les procédures prévues aux articles 49 et 50.

Article 21

Le Premier ministre dirige l'action du Gouvernement. Il est responsable de la Défense nationale. Il assure l'exécution des lois. Sous réserve des dispositions de l'article 13, il exerce le pouvoir réglementaire et nomme aux emplois civils et militaires.
Il peut déléguer certains de ses pouvoirs aux ministres.

Article 34

La loi est votée par le Parlement.
La loi fixe les règles concernant:
– les droits civiques et les garanties fondamentales accordées aux citoyens pour l'exercice des libertés publiques; les sujétions imposées par la Défense nationale aux citoyens en leurs personnes et en leurs biens;
– la nationalité, l'état et la capacité des personnes, les régimes matrimoniaux, les successions et libéralités;
– la détermination des crimes et délits ainsi que les peines qui leur sont applicables; la procédure penale; l'amnistie, la création de nouveaux ordres de juridiction et le statut des magistrats;
– l'assiette, le taux et les modalités de recouvrement des impositions de toutes natures; le régime d'émission de la monnaie.
La loi fixe également les règles concernant:
– le régime électoral des assemblées parlementaires et des assemblées locales;
– la création de catégories d'établissement publics;
– les garanties fondamentales accordées aux fonctionnaires civils et militaires de l'Etat;
– les nationalisations d'entreprises et les transferts de propriété d'entreprises du secteur public au secteur privé.
La loi fixe les principes fondamentaux:
– de l'organisation générale de la Défense nationale;
– de la libre administration des collectivités locales, de leurs compétences et de leurs ressources;
– de l'enseignement;
– du régime de la propriété, des droits réels et des obligations civiles et commerciales;
– du droit du travail, du droit syndical et de la sécurité sociale.
Les lois de finances déterminent les ressources et les charges

de l'Etat dans les conditions et sous les réserves prévues par une loi organique.

Des lois de programme déterminent les objectifs de l'action économique et sociale de l'Etat.

Les dispositions du présent article pourront être précisées et complétées par une loi organique.

Article 37

Les matières autres que celles qui sont du domaine de la loi ont un caractère réglementaire.

Les textes de forme législative intervenus en ces matières peuvent être modifiés par décrets pris après avis du Conseil d'Etat. Ceux de ces textes qui interviendraient après l'entrée en vigueur de la présente Constitution ne pourront être modifiés par décret que si le Conseil constitutionnel a déclaré qu'ils ont un caractère réglementaire en vertu de l'alinéa précédent.

Article 38

Le Gouvernement peut, pour l'exécution de son programme, demander au Parlement l'autorisation de prendre par ordonnances, pendant un délai limité, des mesures qui sont normalement du domaine de la loi.

Les ordonnances sont prises en Conseil des ministres après avis du Conseil d'Etat. Elles entrent en vigueur dès leur publication, mais deviennent caduques si le projet de loi de ratification n'est pas déposé devant le Parlement avant la date fixée par la loi d'habilitation.

A l'expiration du délai mentionné au premier alinéa du présent article, les ordonnances ne peuvent plus être modifiées que par la loi dans les matières qui sont du domaine législatif.

3. Concerning Parliament

Article 28

Le Parlement se réunit de plein droit en deux sessions ordinaires par an.

(*L. const. n° 63-1327 du 30 décembre 1963*) La première session s'ouvre le 2 octobre, sa durée est de quatre-vingt jours.

La seconde session s'ouvre le 2 avril, sa durée ne peut excéder quatre-vingt dix jours.

Si le 2 octobre ou le 2 avril est un jour férié, l'ouverture de la session a lieu le premier jour ouvrable qui suit.

Article 29

Le Parlement est réuni en session extraordinaire à la demande du Premier ministre ou de la majorité des membres composant l'Assemblée nationale, sur un ordre du jour déterminé.

Lorsque la session extraordinaire est tenue à la demande des membres de l'Assemblée nationale, le décret de clôture intervient dès que le Parlement a épuisé l'ordre du jour pour lequel il a été convoqué et au plus tard douze jours à compter de sa réunion.

Le Premier ministre peut seul demander une nouvelle session avant l'expiration du mois qui suit le décret de clôture.

Article 49

Le Premier ministre, après delibération du Conseil des ministres, engage devant l'Assemblée nationale la responsabilité du Gouvernement sur son programme ou éventuellement sur une déclaration de politique générale.

L'Assemblée nationale met en cause la responsabilité du Gouvernement par le vote d'une motion de censure. Une telle motion n'est recevable que si elle est signée par un dixième au moins des membres de l'Assemblée nationale. Le vote ne peut avoir lieu que quarante-huit heures après son dépôt. Seuls sont recensés les votes favorables à la motion de censure qui ne peut étre adoptée qu'à la majorité des membres composant l'Assemblée. Si la motion de censure est rejetée, ses signataires ne peuvent en proposer une nouvelle au cours de la même session, sauf dans le cas prévu à l'alinéa ci-dessous.

Le Premier ministre peut, après délibération du Conseil des ministres, engager devant l'Assemblée nationale la responsabilité du Gouvernement sur le vote d'un texte. Dans ce cas, ce texte est considéré comme adopté, sauf si une motion de censure, déposée dans les vingt-quatre heures qui suivent, est votée dans les conditions prévues à l'alinéa précédent.

Le Premier ministre a la faculté de demander au Sénat l'approbation d'une déclaration de politique générale.

Bibliography

Avril, P., *La Cinquième République: Histoire politique et constitutionnelle*. PUF, 1987.

Constitution française du 4 octobre 1958. © La documentation française. No. 1.04 édition 1993, Secrétariat géneral du gouvernement.

Debré, J.-L., *La Constitution de la Vᵉ République*. PUF, 1975.

Duhamel, O., and J.-L. Parodi, *La Constitution de la Cinquième République*. Presses fond. nat. sciences politiques, 1988.

The French Constitution. Unofficial translation published by the French Embassy in London, Service de Presse et d'Information, 58 Knightsbridge, London SW1X 7JT, January 1986.

Guchet, Y., *La Vᵉ République*. Editions Européennes Erasme, 1990.

Part II:

The Political Parties

General introduction to modern French political parties

N. A. ADDINALL

The examination in Part I of this book of the birth of the Fifth Republic leading to the reduction of the powers of the Parliament whilst increasing those of the president and the government may lead the reader to believe that, as General de Gaulle so vehemently wished, the power of the political parties had largely been destroyed.

In a sense this was true. In the place of the myriad parties of the Fourth Republic, there was, on the one hand, one enormous party – the *Union pour la Nouvelle République* (UNR) – which was composed quite simply of those who were in favour of de Gaulle and his new constitution, and on the other those, principally the Communist and Socialist parties, who were against him.

This polarization had, however, only come about because of the Algerian war, the crisis it provoked, and the conditions for putting an end to it imposed by General de Gaulle. It would therefore be logical to suppose that the ending of the Algerian war on the one hand, and the disappearance of General de Gaulle on the other, would radically change this situation, and bring about the reappearance of the political parties.

Thus it proved. The *Union pour la Nouvelle République* kept its name only until 1962; it then changed it five times between 1962 and 1976 and, whereas the change of name may be considered to some extent cosmetic until 1967, it is clear that by 1976, when Jacques Chirac formed the *Rassemblement pour la République* (RPR), the Gaullist party had undergone a transformation since its early days. This will be examined below in the chapter devoted to the *Rassemblement pour la République*, but it is to be noted here that the centre parties of the Fourth Republic did not disappear – they merely hid under the umbrella of the UNR, together with various Socialists (*les*

Gaullistes de gauche) and even Communists until it was deemed safe for them to come out into the open again.

The resignation of General Charles de Gaulle as president of the Republic on 28 April 1969, and his death the following year, marked a watershed in French politics. Although his former prime minister, Georges Pompidou, was elected on 20 June 1969 to succeed him as president and thereby appeared to assure the continuation of Gaullist policies, it quickly became apparent that Pompidou had far more in common with the traditional values of the centre parties than with the interventionist and state-led policies of de Gaulle. In this he was powerfully aided and abetted by his finance minister, Valéry Giscard d'Estaing, who had also been de Gaulle's finance minister from January 1962 to January 1966, and who, embittered by his dismissal by de Gaulle, had actively encouraged the members of his *Républicains indépendants* party to campaign against de Gaulle's proposals for reform of the *Sénat* and the introduction of decentralization in his referendum of 1969.

When Pompidou died in April 1974, it was not therefore surprising that his successor was Giscard d'Estaing, elected by a narrow majority in the second ballot held on 21 June 1974 against the Socialist, François Mitterrand, whilst the official Gaullist candidate, Jacques Chaban-Delmas, former prime minister (June 1969–July 1972) and mayor of Bordeaux, obtained only 14.6 per cent of the vote in the first ballot.

Since then, political fortunes have waxed and waned, and these are detailed in the History and Development sections devoted to each political party below, but we may note here that by 1974 the Centre had returned to the forefront and was to reinforce its position with the transformation of the *Républicains indépendants* into the *Parti républicain* in May 1977 and, more importantly, with the creation on 1 February 1978 of the *Union pour la démocratie française* (UDF). The latter was a party designed by and for Giscard d'Estaing and is one of the two major parties – the other is the *Rassemblement pour la République* (RPR) – which have constituted the majority in the *Assemblée nationale*, and therefore provided the government, since the general elections of 1993.

This is not to say that the centre parties, and the UDF in particular, have enjoyed unmitigated success from 1974 until 1995. In spite of the fact that they enjoyed considerable reinforcements from 1976 onwards in the form of the support of a new so-called 'Gaullist' party, the *Rassemblement pour la République*, created in that year by

Jacques Chirac, who has twice been prime minister and was elected president of the Republic in May 1995, popular support swung from them to the Socialists during the period 1981–93, with an interlude known as 'cohabitation' between 1986 and 1988.

In spite of the fact that the economic policies of his prime minister, Raymond Barre, had proved most unpopular, and that he himself had been accused by satirical newspapers like the *Canard enchaîné* of such unbecoming behaviour as having accepted presents of diamonds from the Central African emperor and dictator Bokassa, Giscard d'Estaing felt fairly confident of winning the second-round ballot in the presidential elections of 1981 against Mitterrand, the man whom he had already successfully called 'l'homme du passé' when he defeated him in 1974, and who now appeared to be one of nature's losers.

Such confidence was to be misplaced. Giscard did not appear more honest or trustworthy for being young, whilst Mitterrand appeared more likely to incarnate these virtues as a rather older, kindly and more avuncular figure; the new nickname coined for him of 'Tonton' (uncle) was entirely suitable.

Mitterrand it was who won the presidential election in 1981, and he followed up his success by dissolving the *Assemblée nationale* and holding new *élections législatives*, or general elections, which saw a landslide Socialist victory. This massive victory was followed by two years of euphoria during which the Socialist party attempted to carry out its broad programme of social reform and progress, only to come up against severe problems of inflation and balance of payments deficits; these forced it to adopt deflationary 'austerity' measures which, although effective, proved generally unpopular. The foreseeable result was the defeat of the Socialists in the 1986 general elections and the victory of the RPR/UDF alliance.

The Centre/Centre Right was therefore back in power in the sense that it had the majority in the *Assemblée nationale* and the prime minister and the government had therefore to be chosen from its ranks. This is why the prime minister appointed was Chirac, the leader of the majority party in the coalition, the RPR.

At the same time, the president of the Republic was still Mitterrand, the Socialist, since the president, as explained in Part I, is elected for seven years and not five like the *députés* in the *Assemblée nationale*. As we have seen, the powers of the president are basically passive, and there was therefore little that Mitterrand could do to prevent the Chirac government from applying its programme, particularly as far as privatizations were concerned. He could, however, express his dissatisfaction, and he was to find this dissatisfaction increasingly reflected in public opinion as his own popularity grew and that of the government fell; 'Tiens bon, Tonton, on les aura!', he was exhorted by his followers in an Epinal-type image of Mitterrand, the First World War *poilu*, beating back the hordes of Huns. 'Hold on' he did, and he most certainly did 'get them', or Chirac at least, when he defeated the latter in the presidential elections of 1988.

As in 1981, he then dissolved the *Assemblée nationale* and the result of the following elections was a narrow majority for the Socialists and their allies. Successive Socialist governments then followed each other under Michel Rocard, Edith Cresson and Pierre Bérégovoy, all having in common a belief that wealth must be created before it can be redistributed, and that Socialists have a duty to address the hard realities of economics before indulging in utopian dreams of realizing paradise now. The result of such pragmatism, however, was growing disillusionment amongst the voters – if even the Socialist party cannot offer hope for the future, then why bother to vote for it? The result was crushing defeat for the Socialist party in the general elections of 1993, and there were many who felt that defeat was the consequence of the Socialist party having abandoned its position and followed the wrong path; foremost amongst these, no doubt, was Pierre Bérégovoy, the last Socialist prime minister, who – holding himself responsible for the defeat – took his bodyguard's gun and shot himself in the head on the symbolic day of 1 May.

Disillusionment with a Socialist party which appeared to have betrayed its principles may be one of the explanations for the heavy defeat of the Left in the general elections of 1993, but there are others, of which the most plausible is that after twelve years of Socialist rule, broken only by the two-year interlude of cohabitation between 1986 and 1988, people simply felt that it was time for a change.

This explanation did not seem to have occurred to the subsequent RPR/UDF majority, however, which took its landslide win to mean that the population was now in favour of right-wing, *laissez-faire*, economic policies and the rule of market forces. The unrest and the massive demonstrations in France against the government's plans for education and the reform of Air France, in addition to the massive disruption carried out by the fishermen in January and February of 1994, seemed to indicate that public opinion had turned against the Socialists not because they were carrying out left-wing policies but because they were carrying out right-wing ones. The fact that Chirac was elected president of the Republic in 1995 with a programme featuring social welfare measures, whilst Balladur, the incumbent prime minister, was beaten into third place, seems to suggest the same thing.

Do the RPR and the UDF form a monolithic whole, or are there important differences between them? What is their attitude to Le Pen's *Front national*? The point has been made above that the Gaullist party came very close to disappearing with the death of General de Gaulle and this is hardly surprising given that the party was more to do with the man and his stature than with a given set of rigid doctrines. How, therefore, did Chirac manage to revive it when he took it over with the new name of *Rassemblement pour la République* in 1976? The answer to this lies in his dynamic and charismatic personality (lending him an aura of spiritual heir to de Gaulle whereas he was, in fact, a protégé of Pompidou), his attachment to and much-underlined faith in the basic Gaullist concepts of national independence and sovereignty, and his apparent commitment to the Gaullist concept of a 'third way' between capitalism and communism. In fact, as we shall see in the chapter devoted to the RPR, the Chiraquian concept of 'participation' is rather different from that of de Gaulle and contains nothing which Giscard d'Estaing and the UDF could find unacceptable.

In truth, the differences between the RPR and the UDF are largely concerned with national sovereignty and the characters of Chirac and Giscard d'Estaing. As a result of the general elections of 1993 and the presidential elections of 1995, the RPR and Chirac are very much the senior partners, but the two parties have similar policies, attract much the same kind of voter and, in recent years, have formed electoral alliances; at the elections of 1993, for example, they adopted the common name of *Union pour la France*.

The rise of Le Pen's *Front national* since 1984 has appeared to present problems for both the UDF and the RPR but particularly for the RPR whose nationalistic right-wing constitutes a potential clientele for Le Pen's programme of law and order and 'préférence nationale'. The landslide victory of 1993 enabled the RPR/UDF majority not to be reliant on the *Front national* in any way at all but this scenario could change in the future if its popularity continues to grow and if its number of *députés* is increased by the introduction of a system of proportional representation.

Finally, what future – if any – can be envisaged for the Communist party? From being the largest single party in France at the end of the Second World War, the Communist party has seen its power, influence and number of supporters steadily dwindle to such an extent that its political importance has become somewhat peripheral. Whilst some Communists believe that this is just a passing phase, and that the incoherences and contradictions of unbridled capitalism will necessarily bring about its collapse and therefore a return to collective values, it must be doubtful – given the collapse of communist states world-wide – whether communism, at least in an affluent country such as France, is ever likely to return to its former prominent position. We should add that the Communist candidate at the presidential elections of 1995, Robert Hue, gained a higher percentage of votes than expected, but this is probably due to his personality rather than to a revival of the fortunes of the Communist party.

If it fails to recover, the only coherent opposition to the RPR/UDF alliance will be provided by the Socialist party, but as elections during the life of the Fifth Republic have clearly shown, it is extremely difficult for a single party to gain an overall majority. In the absence of a strong Communist party, the Socialist party cannot look to its left for support as it did in June 1972 when it signed the *Programme commun de gouvernement* with the *Parti communiste*, and so it will have to look to the centre. Support from the *Centre des démocrates sociaux* has been forthcoming in the past and may well be so in the future, but it seems more than possible that the *Parti socialiste* will seek to broaden its base by appealing to middle-of-the-road Social Democrats, ecologists, and others who, without holding traditional Socialist views, none the less feel that blind faith in unfettered market forces is not the way forward. Michel Rocard, the former Socialist prime minister, has already expressed a desire to see the formation of such a grouping, and whilst this did not appear to gain the Socialists any votes in the elections of 1993 (and may even have lost them some as appearing to be a betrayal of Socialist beliefs) it is quite possible that such a Social Democrat centre grouping may emerge in the years to come.

Much will no doubt depend on the success or otherwise in office of the RPR/UDF coalition in power from 1993 onwards. If the measures it tries to take prove as unpopular as those it tried to take in education and with Air France, or if disagreements arise between its members, then it may happen that, instead of merging, the RPR/UDF alliance could break up and the political map of the centre could be redrawn. As Giscard d'Estaing points out in his book of the same name, 'deux Français sur trois' have much in common and belong to a socio-economic group which can be situated in the centre. The traditional cleavage between working class and bourgeoisie no longer exists in modern French society and therefore political parties reflecting antagonisms which have largely disappeared should disappear also. 'Deux Français sur trois' therefore belong to a category whose aspirations are best reflected by an intelligent party of the centre, and, whilst Giscard d'Estaing naturally feels that the UDF corresponds to this definition, it is quite clear that the moderate wing of the Socialist party, as represented by Michel Rocard, would also make a claim.

Whether this means that the moderate elements of the Centre and Socialist parties are moving towards the creation of a large Social Democrat-type party remains to be seen, but seems fairly plausible given that the virtual disappearance of the Communist party and the heavy defeat of the Socialists in the 1993 general elections apparently indicate that the population is not looking for left-wing solutions to the country's problems, and although the amount of support for the *Front national* may be viewed as disturbing by many people it is fairly obvious that the extreme Right will never be in a position to provide a viable alternative either. It is perhaps significant that Chirac's victory at the presidential elections of 1995 was due in no small part to the fact that he deliberately occupied the centre-left ground by proposing policies on unemployment and social welfare that had more in common with those of his Socialist second-round adversary, Lionel Jospin, than with those of his fellow member of the RPR, Edouard Balladur. The choice being offered the electorate was therefore no longer the traditional one between the 'Right' and the 'Left'.

1. Le Rassemblement pour la République

N. A. ADDINALL

History and development

It was thought by many that the disappearance of General de Gaulle from the political scene in 1969, and his death the following year, would signify the end of Gaullism. Although the circumstances of the Algerian war had restored him to power in 1958, and the backlash after the 'événements' of 1968 had helped to keep him there, it appeared obvious to many that this was the classic case of the right man coming along at the right time; once the circumstances changed he, and the political doctrines he professed, would disappear.

The very fact that de Gaulle had himself set up a political party in 1947, the *Rassemblement du peuple français*, which he was to outlive (since it ceased to function in 1953), appeared to indicate quite clearly that the man could outlive the ideas, but not the ideas the man.

As noted in the General Introduction, the fortunes of the Gaullist party did not prosper in the years following de Gaulle's death. Although he was succeeded by his former prime minister, Georges Pompidou, and the period 1969–74 was apparently one of harmony and accord between the Gaullists and the supporters of Giscard d'Estaing, it was clear that Pompidou's policies were not those of de Gaulle, but those of the traditional Centre Right.

When Pompidou died in 1974, it was not surprising that the Gaullist pretender to his succession, Jacques Chaban-Delmas, received less than 15 per cent of the votes in the first round, and it was Valéry Giscard d'Estaing who, with the support of Jacques Chirac and other Gaullists, won the battle for the presidency in the second round against François Mitterrand.

It thus appears that, by 1974, the Gaullist party had been largely taken over by the traditional Centre Right, and the sudden cessation between 1971 and 1976 of its regular changing of name is symptomatic of this. Between 1958 and 1971 its title changed from *Union pour la Nouvelle République* (1958) to *Union pour la Nouvelle République–Union démocrate du travail* (UNR–UDT) in 1962, to *Union des démocrates pour la Ve République* (UDV^e) in 1967, to *Union pour la défense de la République* in 1968, and finally – whilst keeping the same format – to *Union des démocrates pour la République* in 1971.

A new element appeared in 1976. As has been observed above, Jacques Chirac supported the candidature of Giscard d'Estaing in the presidential elections of 1974 and was rewarded with the post of prime minister from 1974 to 1976. The two men did not see eye to eye on all issues, however, and in August 1976 Chirac resigned his post, but instead of fading into the background, he decided that he must henceforth play a major role, but at the head of his own party. Instead of trying to create a new party, he decided to rejuvenate the by now fairly moribund UDR by giving it a new name and by claiming the heritage of de Gaulle. On 5 December the name of the party was changed to the *Rassemblement pour la République* (RPR) in a very obvious attempt to recall the consonance of de Gaulle's post-Second World War party, the *Rassemblement du peuple français* (RPF), and Chirac was elected to its presidency.

Since then, the RPR has more than held its own. Although Giscard d'Estaing was the candidate of the Right in the presidential elections of 1981 his defeat at the hands of Mitterrand and subsequent semi-eclipse from the political scene has left the way open for Chirac and the RPR to figure as the dominant partners in the Centre-Right coalition. When this coalition won the general elections of 1986 there was no question but that the prime minister should be the dynamic and charismatic head of the RPR, and Chirac addressed himself to the task of imposing right-wing measures such as privatization and abolition of the wealth tax with a vigour which was to turn public opinion against him by 1988 when the presidential elections were held. The result was victory for Mitterrand and defeat for Chirac, and general elections followed when Mitterrand dissolved the *Assemblée nationale*. In the general election, the Socialist party gained a small majority.

This appeared to represent a fairly serious setback to Chirac himself, if not to the RPR, and his authority over his party was then challenged by '*rénovateurs*' such as Philippe Seguin, who openly opposed him over the Maastricht Treaty. Although he more than survived the challenge, there being a majority within both the party and the country in favour of Maastricht, Chirac did not appear to be in total control of his party until the landslide victory of the RPR/UDF in the general elections of March 1993. Whilst this victory appeared to have more than restored him to a dominant position as head of the senior party in a two-party coalition enjoying an enormous majority, it also presented him with considerable problems.

Chirac's objective was to be the candidate of the Right in the presidential elections of 1995, and to win those elections. This called for considerable popular support from the population as a whole which could be achieved only in one of two ways: either by accepting reappointment as prime minister as in 1986–8, but trying to take only very popular measures this time in order to avoid re-creating the scenario of 1988, or by retiring to the sidelines in Olympian fashion and watching one of his aides try to carry out the task and carry full responsibility if the policies carried out proved to be as unpopular as in 1986–8. Chirac, understandably enough, chose the latter course, leaving it to Balladur, as prime minister, to carry responsibility for the policies of privatization and austerity which the government was committed to applying.

Right up until the results of the first ballot of the presidential elections became known, however, Chirac must have wondered increasingly whether this course had been a wise one. Balladur not only showed himself to be extremely adept at his task, stressing the need for 'sacrifices' to be made whilst at the same time avoiding major conflict and resisting the temptation to accelerate the pace of privatization, he also presented an image of an educated and well-mannered aristocrat who proved increasingly popular as prime minister. When he decided to stand for the presidential elections against Chirac, his friend of thirty years' standing, there were many who thought (and their number increased with every opinion poll) that he was bound to win. Whilst displaying an outward appearance of smiling nonchalance and quiet confidence, Chirac himself must have wondered if he had not made a mistake, if he had not made himself the man of the past and Balladur the 'coming man'.

As it happened, the increasing popularity of the Socialist candidate, Lionel Jospin, gained him the greatest number of votes in the first ballot,[1] mainly at the expense of Balladur who finally only

---

[1] Jospin obtained 23.31% of the vote against Chirac's 20.73% and Balladur's 18.54%.

managed to come third, leaving Jospin and Chirac to fight out the second ballot between them. This was finally won by Chirac with a fairly clear majority, but he had come very close to losing everything to a man who was a member of his own party and whom he had, in effect, appointed prime minister. If Balladur had achieved his ambition of becoming president of the Republic, it would have become very difficult to discern any significant differences between the policies of the RPR and the UDF, Balladur appearing to be very much a man of the same ilk and ideas as the major figures of the UDF, and the two parties might thus have melted into one.

As mentioned in the General Introduction to this volume, Chirac's policies are not far removed from those of the UDF either, but nevertheless, as self-proclaimed inheritor of General de Gaulle, he has had to preach respect for certain doctrines without which one can hardly claim to be Gaullist. These can be summed up as follows:

1. National sovereignty. No country should be under the control of another country, or bloc of countries, any more than any individual should be subservient to another. This is why France, and other countries, should not be dependent militarily on the United States; countries, like individuals, should have free will and be able to decide for themselves.

2. Any country which is dependent on another country economically is also dependent on it politically. It follows that the key sectors of the economy should be kept in national hands and not sold to foreigners.

3. The logical extension of this is that ownership of these key sectors should be by the people via the State, which means nationalization. This is why de Gaulle carried out so many nationalizations at the end of the Second World War.

4. It is imperative that the economy should work efficiently and well in the interests of the nation and it is therefore necessary for the State to plan ahead for the future and provide guidance for the private sector as well as the public sector. Five-year plans are therefore necessary.

5. All of this does not imply that the State becomes all-powerful and the individual disappears. On the contrary, de Gaulle contends that it is the capitalist and communist systems which destroy the individual, the one because of its 'moral infirmity' of putting gain before humanity, the other because of its abject failure to prevent man's exploitation by man. In their place he

proposes a third way which he calls 'participation', and which consists essentially of employees being the shareholders and managers of their own place of employment. As such, they are both employer and employee and thus have the satisfaction of working for themselves as employees instead of for a boss in a capitalist society or the State in a communist one.

Outlined above are the basic themes of Gaullism, as expressed by General de Gaulle. The text below, taken from Chirac's *Discours pour la France à l'heure du choix* covers these themes. Readers will make up their own minds, after reading the passage and answering the questions, whether they think that Chirac remains true to de Gaulle's doctrines, or whether he has attempted to move them somewhat to the right.

Source

Extract from Jacques Chirac, *Discours pour la France à l'heure du choix* (Editions Stock, 1978), pp. 202–11.

. . . Il faut développer dans notre pays une véritable **démocratie du quotidien** par la participation, une démocratie qui doit permettre à chacun de devenir, enfin, le vrai maître de sa vie de tous les jours, de prendre en charge, dans la liberté et dans la responsabilité, l'ensemble des activités, de travail ou de loisir, de la vie courante ou de la vie publique, qui forment, éparses et prosaïques, la matière essentielle de nos travaux et de nos jours.

C'est à l'évidence dans l'entreprise que l'espérance de participation a été jusqu'à présent le plus sensible. C'est là qu'elle a commencé à l'instigation du général de Gaulle, puis de Georges Pompidou,[1] à prendre forme; c'est là qu'elle devra demain, en priorité, s'exercer.

De la création des comités d'entreprise[2] à la reconnaissance de la section syndicale, des ordonnances de 1959 et de 1967 consacrant les droits des salariés sur une partie des fruits de l'expansion jusqu'au

---

[1] Georges Pompidou (1911–74) was prime minister 1962–8 and president of the Republic 1969–74.

[2] *Comités d'entreprise* were created by General de Gaulle. These committees represent management and personnel and are mandatory in businesses with more than fifty employees. They have to be consulted on all matters pertaining to the running of the business, working conditions, training, remuneration, etc.

développement de **l'actionnariat ouvrier**, nous avons conscience d'avoir marché dans la bonne voie et d'avoir préparé le terrain à des transformations plus ambitieuses.

En fait, pour les dix ou quinze années qui viennent, l'interrogation principale, celle qui est au fond du drame de notre siècle, reste la question de la condition ouvrière. Le plus important, et donc le plus difficile, est de transformer non seulement la vie matérielle des travailleurs, mais la condition même des salariés.

A vrai dire, nous sommes ici au cœur du débat fondamental ouvert par les temps modernes. Ce qui compte, ce n'est pas la révolution des mots, mais la transformation des choses. L'histoire nous l'apprend, seules les vraies réformes sont révolutionnaires. C'est-à-dire que notre société ne sera réconciliée avec elle-même, les tensions résolues, les passions purgées, la crise maîtrisée, que dans la mesure où la racine même du mal sera attaquée, les structures transformées et les mentalités rajeunies.

Soyons assurés de ceci: rien ne sera possible (justice, efficacité, liberté) s'il n'existe pas dans l'entreprise un meilleur équilibre quant à la répartition des fruits de l'expansion, quant à l'amélioration des conditions de travail, quant à la juste part de responsabilité que chacun doit se voir attribuer. C'est-à-dire sans un meilleur équilibre des profits, des charges et des responsabilités entre tous les **partenaires sociaux**.

En un mot, les travailleurs doivent être des citoyens de plein droit dans leur entreprise comme ils sont des citoyens de plein droit dans l'Etat républicain. Ils sont conscients de l'importance primordiale de leur activité économique et de leur fonction sociale dans la vie du peuple français. Ils savent quelle part capitale ils ont dans le développement de la puissance économique de notre pays, dans la croissance industrielle française. Ils entendent exercer pleinement leur responsabilité. La participation de tous, de tous les partenaires sociaux, est donc nécessaire à la construction de la nation moderne et à son avenir. Par quel moyen?

Dans notre société, l'expansion en général, le développement d'une entreprise en particulier, sont les résultats d'un effort fait en commun par les **apporteurs de capitaux** et par les **apporteurs de travail**. Il est juste que les résultats de cet enrichissement soient partagés entre tous ceux qui ont concouru à la prospérité de l'entreprise.

En réalité, ce que nous cherchons à faire, c'est à garder l'économie libérale en raison de son irremplaçable valeur de stimulation, mais aussi à la mettre au service d'**une finalité sociale**.

Nous voulons aller à la fois au-delà du socialisme et du capitalisme, c'est-à-dire de leur affrontement.[3] Réussir cette mutation, c'est le rôle du RPR, de ses militants, de ses parlementaires et de ses dirigeants.

Au terme de cet effort, les vieilles habitudes étant brisées, les rapports d'allégeance ayant changé de signification et de nécessité, les intérêts et les responsabilités étant partagés, la pratique de la participation aura transformé les comportements et modifié les mentalités. Et, qui nierait que l'enrichissement et la transformation qualitative des tâches ne soient pas de nature à réconcilier des millions de Français avec le travail en usine et, du même coup, à permettre une amélioration sensible de la situation de l'emploi?

. . . En tout état de cause, nous devons savoir qu'il n'est aucun système de nature strictement juridique qui puisse assurer à lui seul, dans notre pays, l'avènement d'une participation véritable. Il s'agit là d'une affaire essentielle et complexe: autant que la loi elle-même, ce qui sera décisif, c'est la transformation en profondeur des habitudes et des mentalités.

C'est pourquoi nous pensons que la participation ne pourra être réalisée que si l'on multiplie les expériences et que si l'on diversifie les approches. Ce n'est pas parce qu'on favorise l'intéressement aux bénéfices qu'on doit exclure la participation au capital. Ce n'est pas parce qu'on développe à la base les initiatives des travailleurs dans l'organisation des ateliers, la répartition des tâches et la détermination des horaires, que l'on doit pour autant exclure l'information sur les décisions stratégiques engageant l'avenir de l'entreprise. Ce n'est pas parce qu'on développe l'actionnariat ouvrier, que l'on envisage l'institution de 'sociétés d'actionnariat salarié' ou de 'sociétés participatives', chères au président Edgar Faure,[4] que l'on doit pour autant s'interdire toute autre formule.

Cette nécessaire souplesse ne signifie pas, bien entendu, qu'on puisse faire n'importe quoi avec les entreprises françaises.

C'est pourquoi nous récusons l'idée fumeuse de l'autogestion, **cette encombrante utopie** que les socialistes eux-mêmes ne parviennent pas à définir et dont ils ne savent en définitive que

---

[3] Almost identical reproduction of General de Gaulle's ambition as expressed in his *Mémoires d'espoir*.

[4] Edgar Faure (1908–88) was a prominent French politician, several times minister (agriculture, education, social affairs) and prime minister under the Fourth Republic. President of the *Assemblée nationale* 1973–8.

faire.[5] Utopie au demeurant dangereuse, car elle accrédite l'idée que la libération des travailleurs pourrait naître de l'éclatement irrémédiable des cellules fondamentales de la vie économique. Or comment ne pas voir que cet éclatement conduirait inévitablement le pays à la ruine, et par un choc en retour, à la plus implacable des dictatures?

Hors du respect d'un certain nombre de principes essentiels a toute activité économique et à toute vie sociale, la participation ne serait qu'un leurre et qu'une imposture. Elle suppose **une nouvelle distribution des responsabilités mais ne saurait s'accommoder d'une dilution de l'autorité.**

Il doit être clair pour chacun que la participation, c'est le contraire du collectivisme, c'est le contraire de l'anarchie, et c'est le contraire de la démagogie.

Les Français doivent savoir qu'il n'y a pas de participation sans économie de marché et sans liberté d'entreprendre, parce qu'il n'y a pas de partage des bénéfices là où il n'y a plus de bénéfices, et de partage des responsabilités là où le pouvoir a déserté l'entreprise au profit d'une bureaucratie qui lui est extérieure.

. . . Nous sommes conscients que la participation manquerait à sa mission, et trahirait l'espérance qu'elle a fait naître, si elle devait se limiter à la seule sphère de l'entreprise. Notre ambition doit être plus vaste: c'est non seulement la vie de l'entreprise, mais celle de l'économie tout entière qui doit être placée sous le signe de la participation.

Nul doute à cet égard qu'une attention toute particulière doive être portée à la planification, dont il est capital qu'elle redevienne, dans ses objectifs comme dans ses méthodes, le moyen par excellence de la participation collective des Français à la détermination et à la réalisation de leur propre avenir. Au départ, c'est-à-dire à la Libération,[6] le Plan a été le ressort privilégié du décollage économique de la nation: dans un pays dévasté par la guerre, dans une société résolue à la modernisation, dans une économie trop archaïque et trop appauvrie pour que le marché puisse y jouer vraiment son rôle, le Plan a été, pour la France, la charte de l'espérance, l'expression de la volonté et l'instrument du succès.

Depuis lors, l'esprit de la planification s'est peu à peu altéré: l'ouverture des frontières et le dynamisme retrouvé du marché intérieur

---

[5] Chirac's attitude to *autogestion* is obviously very different from Rocard's, whose brainchild it is.

[6] Chirac is referring, of course, to the *Libération* of France in 1944.

ont très salutairement redonné au jeu de l'offre et de la demande un rôle éminent dans l'organisation de la vie économique. Dans le même temps, les ambitions des planificateurs se sont élargies très sensiblement, mais cet élargissement, au lieu de renforcer le Plan, lui a fait perdre son ancienne raison d'être et sa première légitimité : se mêlant de tout et ne tranchant plus en dernier ressort de rien, le Plan a peu à peu cessé d'être un véritable instrument d'action pour devenir une sorte de miroir prospectif que la société se tendrait à elle-même tous les cinq ans.

Je dis qu'aujourd'hui, la page de la croissance facile étant tournée, nous devons aborder une troisième étape et faire du Plan autre chose que la musique d'accompagnement d'une expansion ralentie.

Il ne saurait s'agir à cet égard de substituer une planification autoritaire aux mécanismes de l'économie du marché, mais au contraire de corriger les défaillances propres à ces mécanismes et de restaurer les conditions d'une liberté vraie de l'économie.

Nous constatons, en effet, que le libéralisme traditionnel est aujourd'hui en crise, que ses vieilles recettes, mêmes rajeunies par la révolution keynésienne,[7] sont impuissantes à provoquer le retour à un équilibre de plein emploi. Ecartelées entre les périls de l'inflation, de la banqueroute commerciale, du chômage et de la stagnation, nos sociétés sentent bien que les choses comme elles sont ne peuvent plus durer et que l'avenir ne sera pas taillé dans la même étoffe que le passé.

Il n'y a pas d'avenir digne de ce nom pour l'économie française dans le cadre d'un système de propriété et de décision à la fois collectiviste et centralisé, mais nous ne pouvons nous résigner à voir dans la montée du chômage, dans le développement de l'inflation, dans le déséquilibre de notre balance des paiements, les signes d'une fatalité que seule une cure permanente et générale de sous-emploi de notre appareil productif permettrait de rendre techniquement supportable.

J'ai, pour ma part, la conviction qu'on peut demander au peuple français d'importants efforts et de grands sacrifices, pour peu qu'on lui ouvre dans le même temps des perspectives sérieuses de redressement. Rien n'est plus contraire à une mobilisation vraie des énergies que le consentement préalable des gouvernants à un avenir une fois pour toutes réputé imprévisible.

---

[7] A reference to the famous economist John Maynard Keynes (1883–1946) who taught that governments can prevent unemployment by a redistribution of income enabling the poorest classes to maintain a purchasing power which in turn maintains production and thereby employment.

Nous pensons, quant à nous, que le premier devoir des responsables, c'est de prévoir aujourd'hui ce que sera la gestion de demain, et nous estimons que le Plan sera l'instrument de cette prise de conscience qui, pour être légitime, doit être l'affaire de la nation tout entière.

C'est, à l'évidence, le Plan qui fournit le cadre politique de cette concentration globale. Pour peu qu'on le réforme dans son organisation et dans ses méthodes, il doit permettre une meilleure confrontation des aspirations des acteurs sociaux et devenir ainsi l'instrument d'un renouvellement périodique du contrat social.[8]

A nos yeux, une chose est claire: il ne peut pas y avoir, dans la conjoncture présente, de relance de la politique contractuelle si celle-ci n'est pas assortie d'une redéfinition d'un Plan pour la nation, par la nation.

Questions on the source text

1. What do you understand by *démocratie du quotidien*?
2. Explain the meaning of *l'actionnariat ouvrier*.
3. Who are the *partenaires sociaux*?
4. Who are the *apporteurs de capitaux* and the *apporteurs de travail*? Are their interests the same?
5. What do you understand by *une finalité sociale*?
6. Explain the meaning of *sociétés d'actionnariat salarié* and *sociétés participatives*.
7. Chirac dismisses *autogestion* as *cette encombrante utopie*. Do you see any major difference between *autogestion* and *participation*?
8. Chirac says that *participation* means *une nouvelle distribution des responsabilités mais ne saurait s'accommoder d'une dilution de l'autorité*. What do you think he means by this?
9. Chirac claims that *participation* can only exist in a market economy. What are his reasons for thinking this? Do you agree with them?
10. What was the importance of State planning at the end of the Second World War, and what, for Chirac, should be its role in the future?

---

[8] Perhaps an indirect reference to the *Contrat social* of Jean-Jacques Rousseau (1712–78).

Subjects for further discussion

1. Chirac claims that his version of *participation* will improve the unemployment situation and make millions of French people happier with factory work. To what extent would you agree that his optimism is justified?
2. Do you think that Chirac's ideas have more in common with left-wing political thought than with right-wing political thought?

Biography of Jacques Chirac

Jacques Chirac was born in Paris on 29 November 1932. He is married to Bernadette de Courcel and has two children. Like other prominent French politicians he is a graduate of the prestigious *Ecole nationale de l'administration* (ENA).

Elected as a member of Parliament (*député*) for the Gaullist UDR in Corrèze in 1967 and general secretary of this party in December 1974, he formed, and became president of, the *Rassemblement pour la République* (RPR) in December 1976. He was mayor of Paris from 25 March 1977 until he appointed Jean Tibéri as his successor in May 1995.

He has occupied the posts of secretary of state for employment (1967–8), economy and finance (1968–71), minister in charge of relations with the Parliament (1971–2), minister for agriculture (1972–4) and minister of the interior (1974). He has also twice been prime minister, under President Giscard d'Estaing from May 1974 to August 1976, and under President Mitterrand from March 1986 to May 1988. During this period he carried out a programme of privatization which remained unfinished when he ceased to be prime minister and which was not reversed by the succeeding Socialist government (this latter preferring, from 1988 onwards, a mixed economy to the outright nationalizations of its 1981 predecessor). This programme was such, however, as to convince at least part of the electorate that he had perhaps more in common with Mrs Thatcher than with General de Gaulle.

He has also three times been a candidate for the presidency of the Republic, in 1981, 1988 and 1995. On the first occasion he was eliminated in the first ballot, on the second he was defeated by François Mitterrand in the second ballot and on the third he defeated Lionel Jospin to become the fifth elected president of the Fifth Republic.

Bibliography

Avril, P., *Essais sur les partis politiques*. Payot, 1991.

Calderon, D., *La Droite française*. Editions sociales, 1985.

Charlot, J., *Le Gaullisme d'opposition*. Fayard, 1983.

Chirac, J., *Discours pour la France à l'heure du choix*. Editions Stock, 1978.

——, *La Lueur de l'espérance*. Table Ronde, 1978.

——, *Oui à l'Europe*. Albatros, 1984.

——, *Une nouvelle France, réflexions 1*. Nil editions, 1994.

——, *La France pour tous*. Nil editions, 1994.

Cotta, M., *Les Secrets d'une victoire*. Flammarion, 1995.

de Gaulle, C., *Mémoires d'espoir*. Plon, 1971.

Desjardins, T., *Les Chiraquiens*. Table Ronde, 1986.

——, *L'Homme qui n'aime pas les dîners en ville*. Hachette, 1995.

Domenach, N., *De si bons amis*. Plon, 1994.

Duverger, M., *Le Système politique français*. PUF, 1990.

Giesbert, F.-O., *Jacques Chirac*. Seuil, 1995.

Hanley, D. L., A. P. Kerr and N. H. Waites, *Contemporary France: Politics and Society since 1945*. Routledge and Kegan Paul, 1979.

Nay, C., *Le Dauphin et le régent*. Grasset, 1994.

For more general works on the political parties, see also the bibliographies for the other chapters, particularly those devoted to the *Union pour la démocratie française* and *Le Front national*.

2. L'Union pour la démocratie française

G. F. EVANS

History and development

Like most of the other major political groups in present-day France, the *Union pour la démocratie française* (UDF) is a product of the 1970s. It came into being just before the parliamentary elections of 1978. It took its name from Valéry Giscard d'Estaing's 'visionary' presidential essay of 1976, *Démocratie française*, and was intended to give weight and support to the then president by acting as a counter-force to the Gaullist element in the centre-right parliamentary majority. This had become all the more pressing since Chirac's re-invigorating reorganization of Gaullism and his creation of the RPR (in 1976) which had scored an important victory over its partners/rivals by winning the Paris elections, thereby giving its leader a power base in the capital. On the basis of these beginnings the UDF has come to be seen, not always accurately, as the party of Giscard, and it remains the vehicle for his continuing political presence, especially since he took over the party presidency from Jean Lecanuet in 1988. Despite the clamour of a younger generation of political aspirants, Giscard can still claim to be the most powerful voice of the non-Gaullist right.

Nevertheless, the origins of the UDF reveal it to be not so much a single-minded party with a completely uniform set of principles and beliefs and a strong grass-roots mass support, but more a sometimes tense collection of political forces and personalities which are often the depositories of distinct ambitions and traditions (opportunist conservatives, social democrats, Catholic democrats, anti-clerical secular republicans, and so on).

At the outset, this coalition put together for electoral purposes was made up of a number of separate centrist and right-of-centre parties and groupings which, despite their professions of alliance, did not always sit well together. First there was the *Parti républicain* (PR), itself only recently founded (in 1977) by Giscard himself as a new incarnation of the 1966 *Fédération nationale des républicains indépendants*, the Giscard-led pro-de Gaulle breakaway group of the older conservative *Centre national des indépendants et paysans* (CNIP) which had initially, in 1962, called itself the *Républicains indépendants*. Giscard had retained the presidency of this party until he passed it on in 1982 to the 'coming man', François Léotard, in the wake of his own presidential election defeat. Léotard's difficulties with the judiciary in 1994–5 meant that he was obliged to hand over the presidency, in theory temporarily, to Gérard Longuet. Next there was the *Centre des démocrates sociaux* (CDS), constituted in 1976 as the heir to the Christian Democrat movement which had existed under various names (*Mouvement républicain populaire, Centre démocratie et progrès* and *Centre démocrate*) from the 1940s to the 1970s. Its original president, Jean Lecanuet, handed over to Pierre Méhaignerie in 1982. Periodically this 'party' refuses to form part of the UDF group in the National Assembly. The third group, the *Parti radical* led from 1972 to 1975 by the effervescent, if politically lightweight, Jean-Jacques Servan-Schreiber (known popularly as JJSS), was composed of right-of-centre elements of the old Radical party following the 1972 split in its ranks and the creation of the *Mouvement des radicaux de gauche* by those of its members who were more favourably disposed to the left-of-centre's common programme for government. Within the *Parti radical*'s ranks were different groups distinguished largely by their closeness to or distance from Chirac's Gaullism. In 1983 the leadership of the *Parti radical* passed into the hands of André Rossinot (a supporter of Raymond Barre in 1986), who passed it on to Yves Galland (a 'chiraquien') in 1988. Added to these parties are the Giscardian *Clubs perspectives et réalités*, the first of which was set up in 1965, the Giscardian youth and student organizations, a right-wing splinter group of the *Parti socialiste*, and the individuals who wished to be members of the UDF without joining any of the constituent organizations (the so-called 'adhérents directs').

From these origins, and to a greater degree than most modern 'broad-church' political parties, the UDF has had to navigate between the Charybdis of self-induced dissolution and the Scylla of electoral disaster. The UDF was (and is) divided not only on questions related to the nature of the links between its constituent parts, but also on issues concerning its response to Gaullism and to the general polarization of politics which has taken place during the Fifth Republic. Centrists have traditionally been more resistant to such polarization and more open to consensus politics. As recently as 1988 some UDF politicians, now less fearful of Communists and more fearful of Le Pen's *Front national* party, were tempted to cross the great divide to join the Rocard government's much heralded drive towards 'l'ouverture', and the centrists formed an autonomous group in the National Assembly. But few voters followed. For this simple reason the UDF leadership has had fairly consistently to preach the virtues of co-operation to the right. Giscard's analysis of Mitterrand's success pin-pointed the latter's ability to hold his own coalition together while sowing dissension in the ranks of the Centre Right. In bald electoral terms, the experience of the 1980s and 1990s would seem to confirm this: the Centre Right divided has failed, the Centre Right united has succeeded. Both the 1986 and 1993 'cohabitations' were brought about by the strategy of union, and, in a report filed in *Le Monde* of 21 November 1992, Giscard is shown looking ahead to the 1995 presidential election with the announcement to the UDF National Council that a single Centre Right candidate is a necessary condition for success:

> Nous avons vécu trop intensément depuis douze ans les dommages causés à notre pays par une présidence socialiste pour imaginer de prendre la responsabilité du retour d'une pareille aventure. Aussi je vous annonce qu'il n'y aura qu'un seul candidat de l'opposition au premier tour de la prochaine élection présidentielle. (p. 10)

In the event the UDF itself would not provide such a candidate. This, like the fact that the UDF survived the loss of the presidency and the initial failures of its partner to regain it, may however say as much about the competing fortunes of the other major political movements and the UDF's relationship with them as it does about the quality of the mortar responsible for holding its constituent parts together.

Electoral fortunes

One of the highlights in the life of the UDF preceded its birth – the election of Giscard as president of the Fifth Republic in the elections made necessary by the death of Georges Pompidou in 1974. Voting patterns, however, make it clear that this could never have happened had not the Gaullist camp been split, with some of their support going to Giscard rather than to the official Gaullist candidate, Jacques Chaban-Delmas. The latter could only muster 14.6 per cent of the first-round votes – as opposed to Giscard's 32.6 per cent – before the Right reunited to prevent the election of a left-wing president. The new president was still left with Gaullists holding the upper hand in parliament. Indeed, the gap between the president and the coalition which was responsible for his election widened throughout his presidency.

A truer reflection of the UDF's own support came, promisingly, in the first parliamentary elections that it fought in its own name. In these 1978 elections it obtained a worthy 20.4 per cent of the first-ballot vote (as against the Gaullists' 22.4 per cent), showing that it could not be regarded as a truly minor partner in the Right coalition. This coalition retained its majority, thereby putting off the 'evil day' of a Socialist party victory a little longer. The UDF vote held up in consequent elections, but only once – in 1988 in the wake of the failure of Chirac's presidential campaign – has the UDF managed to win a larger percentage of the popular vote and a greater number of parliamentary seats than its RPR partner/rival. And even this was relatively short-lived, the RPR reversing this outcome in the 1993 parliamentary elections which saw the Right coalition gain a landslide victory with the UDF itself gaining more votes than the outgoing party of government, the Socialist party. Be that as it may, the UDF has never once approached the peaks of parliamentary electoral performance reached by the Gaullists in the late 1960s or by the Socialists in the 1980s when percentages of the vote in the upper thirties were recorded. On this basis, the UDF has never been in a position to dominate the political scene or to make claims to be the 'natural party of government'. In addition, the failure of the UDF to find a convincing new leadership other than Giscard increases the chances of it breaking up. Yet it won, and retains, sufficient electoral clout to ensure that it cannot be ignored. While it has not managed to replace Gaullism nor even to 'Giscardize' it, it succeeded in making Gaullism dependent on it for government. This dependence is, however, double-edged. Although it has its own strength in European and French regional politics, the UDF, an at times uneasy coalition itself, still needs to be part of an even wider coalition of the Centre Right if it is to have any real impact on French domestic politics at the national level. Hence its relative weakness despite its relative strength.

Principles and policies

The founding principles of the UDF have to be set in the context of the general centrist political strategy needed to respond to political realities, namely the obligation to work with, but remain distinct from, the post-de Gaulle Gaullist Right, while at the same time facing up to the challenge of the increasingly united Left. These pressures had produced the slogans used by Giscard in his bid for the presidency in 1974 – 'Continuité et ouverture' (in round one) and 'le changement sans risque' (in round two). These slogans were attractively balanced in electoral terms (underlining as they did the eagerness for change but rejecting complete reversal and disruption), even if they were intellectually unexciting, even vacuous. Giscard's two main statements of principle, *Démocratie française* (1976, while he was in office) and *Deux Français sur trois* (1984, when he was seeking to rebuild his career after losing the presidency), were meant to fill the vacuum and put flesh on the bones of the 'réformisme collectif' which Giscard had publicly committed himself to since the 1960s. At the heart of this enterprise lay the effort to redefine in a French context a modern 'liberalism' in political, social and economic senses, which would have a more human face than allowed by its usual right-of-centre meanings in France and would effectively counter the competing attractions and principles of the Left. In this way Giscard sought to create the space for a third-way consensus which could underpin his own position. In the process he was obliged to admit that 'notre histoire a enraciné [. . .] dans l'opinion publique le concept d'une liberté politique dressée contre le pouvoir, et celui d'une liberté économique s'accompagnant d'abus et servant à consolider les inégalités sociales' (*Deux Français sur trois*, chap. IV). This would explain the constant to-and-fro in Giscard's essays between affirmation and negation, and the fact that the most important recurrent themes are 'prospective' rather than 'conservative'.

These themes include the insistence that the social changes already under way in France need to be matched with new political and economic principles more appropriate than those of either the traditional Left or the traditional Right (thereby staking Giscard's claim to be 'modern' and 'forward looking' without being extremist). Thus Giscard gives support to economic liberalism, but not in its antisocial forms; he is critical of socialist-style intervention and planning, but makes the state responsible for protecting its citizens against those calamities which are beyond their individual control; he claims that industrial success will be undermined by nationalization and/or workers' control, but will depend on worker participation and scope for initiative. It is also stressed that if the legitimate, competing demands of individual freedom and self-fulfilment and collective national success are to be met within a democratic framework, then the key will be found in the principle of pluralism. However, 'ce pluralisme ne saurait être seulement politique: il doit être total' (*Démocratie française*, Troisième Partie). In other words, pluralism must not only extend to all of the country's internal institutions and organizations, which involves demonopolizing and decentralizing the powers of the state, parties, unions, media, and so on, but will also increasingly affect the country's attitudes to Europe, the United States, *détente* and the Third World.

Converting such general principles into detailed policy is, of course, a fraught business. However, the main thrust of UDF action (in office) and pronouncement (out of office) has arguably been in line with the guiding principles outlined by Giscard, even if there are occasions when the need to collaborate with the RPR or, later, to deal with the unsettling competition of the *Front national*, internal political rivalries (such as that between Giscard and Barre) and the pressures of external political and economic events may distract from, even frustrate, their fulfilment.[1] So, while it may be right to point out divisions between the constituent parties of the UDF, especially when out of power,[2] and the existence of pretty illiberal elements within the Giscardian ranks (as witness the interventions of Poniatowski on the immigration issue), it is no doubt an exaggeration to claim that the UDF has 'no strong policy commitments'.[3] Certain constants do keep surfacing, even if they have to be adapted to changing circumstances – itself less of a problem for a future-orientated party. For example, in the run-up to the 1993 parliamentary elections, the UDF produced

---

[1] For instance, France's poor energy situation after the oil price rises of the 1970s ensured UDF support for strong state intervention and control in the nuclear energy field.

[2] See, for example, F. Borella, *Les Partis politiques dans la France d'aujourd'hui* (5ᵉ éd., Seuil, 1990): 'le clivage au sein de l'UDF passe entre ceux qui dénoncent les dangers des politiques de redistribution et de justice sociales . . . et ceux qui les estiment indispensables pour la réalisation du bien commun ou de l'intérêt général' (p. 124).

[3] John Frears, *Parties and Voters in France* (Hurst & Co., London, 1991), p. 42.

its 'new social pact' for discussion with its RPR electoral allies.[4] This numbered among its main clauses a new wave of decentralization measures, including offering greater autonomy for schools in the national education system (now in the name of respect for 'subsidiarity'), the completion of European Monetary Union, the democratization of the European electoral system and support for further privatizations. All of these could be said to be perfectly consistent with the initial UDF prospectus laid out in Giscard's earlier works. Indeed, Giscard's presidential election slogans would appear to live on. Whether that can ever again be an electoral advantage for the UDF is, however, a moot point, especially since it looks as if first Balladur then Chirac sought to hijack the appeal to consensus politics.

Sources

Text A: From the Preface to V. Giscard d'Estaing, *Démocratie française* (Librairie Arthème Fayard, 1976; Livre de poche edition, 1978)

Qu'affirme, en effet, *Démocratie Française*?

Il n'est pas facile de condenser en cinquante lignes un ouvrage déjà conçu comme un résumé. Tentons-le cependant:

– au stade déjà atteint de son développement, la société française doit être organisée à partir de l'homme et pour l'homme. Ni **le libéralisme classique**, ni le marxisme, conçus à des stades antérieurs, ne fournissent de modèles satisfaisants;

– le problème à résoudre aujourd'hui n'est pas celui d'une coupure permanente de la société française, ni celui de **la lutte des classes**. Certes les Français demeurent et demeureront divisés en plusieurs idéologies. Mais, à l'instar de ce qui s'est passé dans les autres démocraties industrielles, la croissance a favorisé le développement d'un vaste groupe central, déjà majoritaire, caractérisé par un comportement, un mode de vie, une éducation, une information, une culture et des aspirations qui tendent à devenir homogènes. L'existence de ce groupe et son évolution, dont la lutte des classes ne rend pas compte, est une donnée majeure de la réalité sociale.

Cette unification progressive de la société française doit être facilitée par la recherche exigeante d'une plus grande justice, ce qui

---

4   See the report in *Le Monde* of 21 November 1992.

ne signifie ni l'uniformisation, ni le nivellement. Les résultats observables dans la lutte contre la misère, les handicaps, les privilèges, et les inégalités de chance culturelles, jalonnent la voie à suivre;

 – notre société s'assignant comme objectif l'épanouissement de l'individu, une organisation collectiviste de la société, déjà contraire aux exigences de l'efficacité, le serait aussi aux aspirations de notre peuple. Cependant l'option en faveur de l'individu doit être rendue compatible avec la construction d'une société de participation et de communication, et avec celle d'une communauté plus fraternelle, dans la vie de travail et dans la cité;

 – le commun dénominateur, le fil d'Ariane de ces recherches est l'idée d'autonomie et de responsabilité. Ce fil directeur nous conduit à une conception pluraliste de l'organisation sociale;

 – **le pluralisme** ne se fragmente pas. On ne peut pas vouloir conserver le pluralisme dans le domaine politique, tout en l'éliminant dans les autres domaines. Car ce n'est pas seulement le pouvoir de l'Etat, mais aussi le pouvoir économique, celui des organisations de masse, celui des moyens d'information, qui contiennent en germe des risques de domination. Il est essentiel que ces pouvoirs ne soient pas confondus entre eux, ni accaparés par une seule organisation.

Voilà pour les principes.

Mais il ne s'agit pas seulement d'énoncer des principes. Leur mise en œuvre concrète s'en déduit directement.

D'abord, de façon négative, évitons de choisir des moyens qui aillent à l'encontre des fins.

Par exemple, si nous voulons que l'individu soit davantage maître de son sort, et libre de prendre un nombre croissant de décisions, il ne faut pas:

 – accroître les pouvoirs ou les dimensions d'une administration déjà tentaculaire;

 – **nationaliser les entreprises** qui n'assument pas un service public, ce qui **conduirait inévitablement, soit à les livrer à la technocratie, soit à les étatiser** et à les faire diriger par quelques fonctionnaires d'administration centrale non responsables;

 – **planifier** autoritairement **l'économie**, ce qui reviendrait à donner à quelques hommes le pouvoir de décider pour plusieurs millions;

 – supprimer l'initiative et la concurrence.

En termes positifs, il faut, au carrefour, choisir *une autre voie*:

 – approfondir les libertés: non seulement les libertés politiques

fondamentales, mais aussi les libertés nouvelles de la vie quotidienne, comme la liberté de l'enseignement, du choix médical, de l'information;
- conserver **l'économie de marché**, seule manière d'assurer la responsabilité des dirigeants et des cadres, et l'efficacité de l'entreprise:
- décentraliser hardiment, dans l'entreprise, et vers la vie locale;
- créer de nouvelles formes de vie, d'urbanisation, de loisirs, de culture. Donner une dimension qualitative à la croissance économique, pour en faire une *croissance douce*.

De même que la philosophie cherche une nouvelle philosophie, de même la politique, longtemps surplombée par les statues écrasantes et raidies du marxisme et du capitalisme triomphant, chemine vers une *nouvelle politique*.

Text B: 'La Société à partir de l'homme' from chap. IV,
***Démocratie française* (Livre de poche edition, 1978), pp. 86–9**

Dans la vie professionnelle, l'organisation sociale doit favoriser l'épanouissement et non l'écrasement de la personnalité. Tâche qui commence avec la possibilité de choisir sa profession grâce à une éducation de niveau culturel élevé et intelligemment orientée; qui implique l'amélioration de la sécurité et des conditions de travail; qui appelle **le développement des expériences**, encore timides, d'enrichissement des tâches et d'organisation **d'équipes autonomes**; qui nécessite la 'seconde chance' offerte par **la formation permanente**, moins pour rectifier une erreur de départ que pour généraliser une chance de promotion; qui suppose enfin, à côté du travail salarié, le développement d'un large secteur de travail indépendant, souvent plus 'gratifiant' par les libertés et responsabilités qu'il comporte.

Cette conception se situe, elle aussi, à l'opposé du collectivisme. C'est évident pour le travail indépendant. Reconnaître dans la situation de **celui qui**, agriculteur, artisan, ou commerçant, **se met 'à son compte'**, non la survivance d'un âge dépassé, mais une forme valable d'accomplissement et de promotion, c'est prendre le contrepied du collectivisme. Ce que l'on sait de l'organisation collectiviste des fonctions agricole, artisanale et commerciale atteste la faillite du système dans ces domaines.

Il en va de même pour le travail salarié. Les nécessités techniques qui ont conduit, quels que soient les régimes, à la constitution **de grands établissements industriels ou tertiaires** dans certains secteurs définis de l'économie, impliquent l'existence de puissantes structures collectives, tant de la part des entreprises que des travailleurs.

Mais si l'on choisit de favoriser le développement de l'individu, il ne faut pas le laisser laminer par ces structures. Il est indispensable de maintenir la liberté de choisir son entreprise, de quitter celle-ci pour entrer dans celle-là, sans l'autorisation de personne. Aucun appareil ou administration ne doit contrôler l'embauche ou la promotion.

D'une façon générale, le remède à ce qu'il y a de trop pesant pour l'individu dans la vie industrielle moderne ne doit pas être cherché dans une organisation plus pesante encore, comme le serait une structure collectiviste. Mais dans la protection et le développement de toutes les libertés individuelles des travailleurs.

Notre société se fonde sur *la responsabilité de l'individu*.

La sécurité n'est pas **le sécurisme**, mais la mise en place, partout, d'un plancher de sécurité, c'est-à-dire de garanties minimales, aussi élevées que possible, et au-delà desquelles s'exercent l'initiative et la responsabilité individuelles.

Notre époque a vu le développement rapide d'institutions destinées à protéger chacun contre les risques majeurs de l'existence: maladie, chômage, vieillesse.

Cette évolution est positive. Une des injustices de la société d'autrefois était de faire subir par l'individu les conséquences d'événements ou de situations sur lesquels il n'avait pas de possibilité d'agir.

Cette sécurité et cette protection contre l'insurmontable doivent être encore améliorées et étendues. Les actions déjà évoquées, dont le but est de mettre tout Français à l'abri de la misère, vont dans ce sens. La garantie de 90% de leur salaire brut aux chômeurs victimes d'**un licenciement économique**, mise en place depuis deux ans, constitue également un progrès de la société. De même, la **généralisation de la Sécurité sociale** à tous les Français, décidée pour le 1er janvier 1978, couronnera cinquante années d'évolution. Elle correspond à une nécessité.

Mais il doit y avoir une limite à cette prise en charge collective dans une société tournée vers l'épanouissement de l'homme. Les abus relevés dans certains cas d'indemnisation du chômage ou dans le fonctionnement de l'assurance-maladie, pour ne citer que ces deux exemples, illustrent cette nécessité. Autant il est justifié de garantir l'être humain contre des événements qui le dépassent, autant il est pernicieux de le dispenser de sa part d'effort à l'égard des éléments sur lesquels il peut agir, sans s'en remettre à la collectivité.

Certains, tout en se prétendant bruyamment favorables à l'autonomie de l'individu, se font une spécialité de réclamer en toute circonstance des garanties accrues de la part de la collectivité. Ils se gardent bien d'indiquer le prix de ce **'garantisme'**. Sans doute tablent-ils sur la naïveté du public, porté à croire que l'avantage est gratuit, ou que ce sont d'autres qui paieront entièrement pour lui. Cela est évidemment inexact. Actuellement, sans même tenir compte de la part financée par l'impôt, chacun de nous paie les diverses sécurités dont nous avons entouré notre existence par un prélèvement de l'ordre de 35% sur son propre salaire. On peut craindre que, si ce pourcentage devait encore augmenter, l'avantage net pour l'individu n'en soit pas accru, mais réduit. La question se pose objectivement de savoir si la part du traitement ou du salaire sur l'emploi duquel l'individu n'a aucun pouvoir de décision ni d'affectation doit croître indéfiniment sans limite. Ou si, comme nous le pensons, pour protéger l'individu et sa liberté de choix, une limite doit être tracée, au-delà de laquelle la société changerait de nature.

Text C: 'Pluralisme et liberté' from chap. VI, *Démocratie française* (Livre de poche edition, 1978), pp. 109–15

Nous avons souligné l'insuffisance, mais aussi l'actualité de la pensée libérale. L'insuffisance, parce que **le libéralisme classique** ne reconnaît que le pouvoir politique, alors que le pouvoir n'est pas seulement politique, mais économique, social, spirituel. En même temps, l'actualité du libéralisme: tandis que sur plusieurs continents l'expérience montre l'impuissance **des systèmes collectivistes** à permettre une pratique démocratique du pouvoir, la conception libérale de pluralité des pouvoirs confirme sa vitalité.

Elle reçoit aujourd'hui en France l'hommage, prononcé d'un ton un peu forcé, de ceux qui, pendant soixante années, n'ont cessé de la tourner en dérision. Sans doute, la soudaineté du revirement, l'aisance avec laquelle il s'est accompli, jettent un doute sur son authenticité. Mais la reddition intellectuelle qu'il constitue n'en a que plus de signification.

Dans notre partie du monde, il n'y a plus aujourd'hui de conception avouable du pouvoir, que libérale. Prenons-en acte.

Mais les idées exigent d'être pensées jusqu'au bout. Pourquoi l'idée fondamentale, selon laquelle seule une structure pluraliste du pouvoir est compatible avec la démocratie, ne serait-elle vraie que dans l'ordre politique? Pour l'admettre, il faudrait supposer que la sphère du politique est entièrement indépendante des autres: erreur dont Marx a été précisément l'un des premiers à faire justice.

Le pluralisme ne se divise pas. Son application porte sur la société tout entière, et s'étend à chacun des domaines de la vie sociale.

Le pluralisme de la société tout entière implique que les divers pouvoirs à l'œuvre dans nos sociétés ne puissent en aucun cas se confondre, et notamment les quatre types essentiels de pouvoirs que sont: le pouvoir d'Etat, le pouvoir économique, le pouvoir des organisations de masse et le pouvoir de la communication de masse. C'est le sens nouveau que revêt aujourd'hui **la règle de la séparation des pouvoirs**.

Parodiant un mot célèbre, on peut dire que toute société dans laquelle ces pouvoirs ne sont pas séparés ne respecte pas le pluralisme.

Une société authentiquement démocratique doit être intégralement pluraliste. Cette exigence s'étend à chacun des pouvoirs pris séparément.

La structure pluraliste du pouvoir politique suppose évidemment la pluralité des partis et les libertés qui l'accompagnent, mais aussi la *distinction effective des pouvoirs d'Etat*: l'autonomie de l'exécutif par rapport au législatif, telle que la Constitution de la Vᵉ République l'a instaurée et que la majorité l'a respectée, l'indépendance judiciaire, telle que la tradition républicaine l'établit et dont le Président de la République est le garant, indépendance que j'ai scrupuleusement protégée.

Elle implique aussi un *pouvoir local, et d'abord communal*, qui soit réel.

Des siècles de centralisation pèsent sur nous. Nous leur devons **l'hypertrophie parisienne et l'atonie de certaines provinces**, comme aussi le foisonnement de la réglementation, et le développement insuffisant des responsabilités.

Il est contraire au principe libéral du pouvoir de traiter au sommet des questions qui peuvent être réglées à la base. Un puissant mouvement de décentralisation est nécessaire, qui transfère à des collectivités locales revigorées et dotées de ressources financières appropriées, des attributions retenues par l'Etat central.

Qu'on ne s'y méprenne pas. Il ne s'agit pas d'ajouter quelques mesures techniques à celles qui sont déjà intervenues dans ce sens au cours des années passées. Mais bien de viser à un véritable changement de nature dans les rapports respectifs de l'Etat, des collectivités locales et du citoyen.

Bien entendu, en de telles matières, il ne s'agit pas d'imposer des bouleversements. Il faut fixer un objectif à terme réaliste, tel qu'il puisse recueillir un consensus, et conduire vers lui l'évolution. C'est pourquoi **une instance de réflexion de haut niveau** a été constituée, avec la charge de définir la structure souhaitable de notre organisation locale à la fin du xxᵉ siècle, restituant aux collectivités locales les trois éléments du pouvoir que sont les attributions, les moyens et les responsabilités. *Une loi fondamentale devra déterminer les compétences propres de l'Etat, des départements et des communes.*

L'adoption pour Paris d'un statut de plein exercice, mettant fin à cent ans de régime d'exception, prouve qu'en un tel domaine, l'évolution peut être conduite à son terme. La société démocratique aura donné un maire aux Parisiens.

Il restera enfin, pour le niveau supérieur de l'organisation locale, à revoir la répartition des compétences entre le département et la région, la superposition de trois collectivités locales étant excessive, à un moment où viendront s'y ajouter des instances européennes. C'est un choix qu'il faudra effectuer dans quelques années, après un temps raisonnable de mise à l'épreuve loyale et complète des institutions régionales actuelles.

Si importante que soit cette question, elle ne concerne que **les modalités de la décentralisation.** L'essentiel, c'est le principe de la décentralisation lui-même: il doit être appliqué hardiment.

La pluralité nécessaire des *organisations de masse* est officiellement admise aujourd'hui par tous, s'agissant notamment des partis politiques. Ralliement sincère, c'est une autre affaire, mais en tout cas, ralliement.

De même, le pluralisme s'impose dès lors qu'il s'agit de *communication de masse.*

Pluralisme de la presse écrite, qu'il est indispensable de préserver et dont le maintien justifie, dans leur principe, les aides attribuées par l'Etat pour alléger les charges de fabrication **des journaux d'information.** Une réflexion publique, conduite avec l'ensemble des parties intéressées, devra porter sur les moyens de préserver l'indépendance et la pluralité des organes de presse.

Pluralisme aussi des moyens de communication audiovisuels.

L'éclatement de l'ancien office de radio et de télévision en plusieurs sociétés nationales, effectivement indépendantes les unes des autres, contribue à la consolidation de nos libertés. La règle de l'indépendance et de la concurrence doit être développée dans tous ses aspects, en y intégrant l'objectif de qualité culturelle des programmes.

Dans ces domaines, la nécessité du pluralisme n'est réellement pas contestée chez nous, du moins ouvertement. Il suffisait donc de la rappeler. Il en va tout autrement *dans l'ordre de l'économie*.

En effet, depuis plusieurs années, le problème de la nationalisation des grandes entreprises françaises a été placé au cœur du débat politique.

Ici aussi le pluralisme des pouvoirs est indispensable: la multiplication des nationalisations, en mettant toutes les entreprises importantes directement entre les mains du pouvoir politique, affaiblirait bien plus qu'elle ne renforcerait la démocratie.

Le préambule de la Constitution de 1946, auquel se réfère **la Constitution en vigueur**, prévoit la nationalisation des entreprises lorsqu'elles ont le caractère d'un service public national ou d'un monopole de fait. Cette conception a présidé à la plupart des nationalisations effectuées à la Libération. Elle n'a pas à être remise en cause. Tout récemment, elle a conduit le Gouvernement à proposer la nationalisation du service public de l'électricité de la Martinique, de la Guadeloupe, de la Guyane et de la Réunion, à laquelle le législateur de 1945 avait omis de procéder.

Mais loin d'être une panacée, la nationalisation ne doit être envisagée qu'en tout dernier recours, car la multiplication des nationalisations conduit inévitablement à une redoutable concentration du pouvoir économique, puis du pouvoir tout court.

Certes, une nationalisation qui laisse subsister intégralement l'économie de concurrence, comme celle de Renault en 1945, ne modifie pas substantiellement la structure du pouvoir économique. Elle ne change guère, en vérité, que la procédure de désignation des dirigeants.

En contrepartie, elle fait reposer sur le contribuable la charge de l'indemnisation (sauf bien sûr le cas de confiscation) et, pour l'avenir, oblige à remplacer, pour l'apport de capitaux frais, l'épargnant défaillant par le budget.

De plus, l'expérience montre que les entreprises nationales du secteur concurrentiel font peu de profits et paient une faible part de l'impôt sur les sociétés. De telles nationalisations modifient ainsi la répartition du prélèvement fiscal en accroissant la part demandée aux particuliers et aux entreprises demeurées privées.

A cela se limitent, pour l'essentiel, les changements. Mais c'est précisément ce que les partisans du collectivisme critiquent: les nationalisations qu'ils réclament sont à l'opposé de celle de Renault. Elles ont pour but de soustraire les entreprises à la concurrence et de les assujettir à une planification autoritaire, baptisée démocratique.

Cette position a sa logique. A quoi bon multiplier les nationalisations, si c'était pour ne rien changer à la structure du pouvoir économique ni aux principes de la gestion des entreprises?

On voit ainsi que la propriété privée du capital des entreprises n'est pas une singularité anachronique, un détail accessoire du système social. Elle est, au contraire, inhérente à une certaine organisation de l'économie, comportant la concurrence et l'autonomie des entreprises. On ne peut vouloir l'une sans l'autre, comme le montre d'ailleurs, sur la carte de la planète, la répartition de chaque système. Il n'existe pas de pays où l'essentiel des grandes entreprises soit nationalisé, et où subsistent les formes de liberté dont nous nous réclamons.

C'est dire que la nationalisation systématique des grandes entreprises signifie nécessairement le choix d'un système économique profondément différent.

Questions on the source texts

Text A

1. Explain the following:
   (i) *le libéralisme classique*
   (ii) *la lutte des classes*
   (iii) *cette unification progressive de la société française*
   (iv) *le pluralisme*
   (v) *nationaliser les entreprises (. . .) conduirait inévitablement, soit à les livrer à la technocratie, soit à les étatiser (. . .)*
   (vi) *planifier l'économie*
   (vii) *l'économie de marché*
2. (i) Enumerate the main principles outlined in this extract and explain the reasoning behind the principles.

(ii)   In more specific policy terms, what is to be rejected and what is to be supported?

Text B

1. Explain the following:
    (i)   *la vie professionnelle*
    (ii)   *le développement des expériences . . . d'équipes autonomes*
    (iii) *la formation permanente*
    (iv)   *celui qui . . . se met 'à son compte'*
    (v)   *de grands établissements industriels ou tertiaires*
    (vi)   *le sécurisme*
    (vii) *un licenciement économique*
    (viii) *la généralisation de la Sécurité sociale*
    (ix)   *ce 'garantisme'*

2. (i)   What is the overall objective presented for approval in this text, and what is the main target for criticism?
    (ii)   How is individual self-fulfilment to be encouraged?
    (iii) What role has government to play?
    (iv)   Why must some line be drawn when it comes to social security provision?

Text C

1. Explain the following:
    (i)   *le libéralisme classique*
    (ii)   *les systèmes collectivistes*
    (iii) *la règle de la séparation des pouvoirs*
    (iv)   *l'hypertrophie parisienne et l'atonie de certaines provinces*
    (v)   *une instance de réflexion de haut niveau*
    (vi)   *les modalités de la décentralisation*
    (vii) *des journaux d'information*
    (viii) *la Constitution en vigueur*

2. (i)   Why is traditional liberalism no longer satisfactory?
    (ii)   Why is liberalism attracting renewed attention?
    (iii) List the four kinds of power identified by Giscard.
    (iv)   What have been the effects of centralization in France?
    (v)   How radical is Giscard's approach to decentralization?
    (vi)   What has been done to ensure pluralism in the media?
    (vii) What is Giscard's main argument against nationalization?

Biography of V. Giscard d'Estaing

Like the relative strengths and weaknesses of the UDF, Giscard's achievements are both impressive and circumscribed.

In its early stages his political career was marked by great success and a certain inevitability. Born in 1926 into a wealthy Puy-de-Dôme family with finance and politics in its veins, and after a brilliant academic career at both the *Ecole Polytechnique* and the *Ecole nationale d'administration*, the 1950s saw him building a political career on classic lines: Banque de France, Ministère des Finances, membership of the finance minister's 'cabinet', followed by election as a *député* in his grandfather's old constituency in the Puy-de-Dôme and first ministerial appointment as *Secrétaire d'état aux finances*, so becoming the youngest minister in the Fifth Republic. Throughout the 1960s and early 1970s not only did he further his own career through experience in government as finance minister in the Pompidou, Chaban-Delmas and Messmer administrations (1962–6 and 1969–74), but he also laid the foundations for the non-Gaullist Centre Right coalition whose candidate he became for the 1974 presidential election, which he then won.

Given the balance of the forces which brought him to office, Giscard's presidency was always going to be a difficult one. In retrospect, it can be seen that there was a gap between initial ambitions and ultimate achievement. There were, of course, a good number of different reasons for this, political, economic and personal, not all of them within Giscard's control.

First and foremost, the fact that the Gaullists were essential to any overall legislative programme left too many hostages to fortune. Even in the early heady days of the presidency, a number of social reforms which had Giscard's personal backing (the abortion law and liberalizing divorce, for example) were found to need 'opposition' support to get on the statute books. And as relations between the president and his Gaullist 'allies' deteriorated, particularly after Chirac's resignation as prime minister in 1976, the latter's embittered and aggressive desire to frustrate Giscard's projects increased. This meant that many elements of the government's cherished reform programme were trimmed or quietly abandoned in the face of the pressures coming as much from Giscard's own side as from the Left. In the second place, Giscard's presidency was to witness the end of the years of economic plenty, the so-called 'trente glorieuses', and the onset of recessionary crisis which deepened with the advent of the Iranian revolution and the Iran–Iraq war which sent oil prices booming yet again, an effect to which France was peculiarly vulnerable despite Giscard's efforts to increase the domestic nuclear energy output. Inevitably Giscard became associated with all the attendant unpleasant consequences on finance and employment, and with the increasingly disliked insensitivity of the tough deflationary policies followed by his prime minister, Raymond Barre. Finally, Giscard's earlier electoral image as a nice, ordinary, informal family man who was both close to the people and full of highly competent technocratic reforming energy was steadily undermined, to be replaced by a popular perception of an autocratic, aloof, even snooty figure, increasingly timid and conservative and not untouched by personal scandal – such as the president's alleged willingness to take a gift of diamonds from the former despotic head of state of the Central African Empire, the self-proclaimed Emperor Bokassa. Giscard could open his 1981 re-election campaign with claims to have completed successfully his initial mission – in·Servan-Schreiber's account (see *L'Express* of 3 June 1974) Giscard had announced to his new ministers in 1974 that 'nous sommes ici pour changer la France' – but not enough of the electorate was convinced. The achievements of the social reforms, the continued industrial modernization and France's role in the construction of Europe were outweighed by the retreat into austerity, the aggressively renewed Gaullism, the need-for-a-change promise of Mitterrand's Left and the loss of personal appeal.

Giscard was initially so hard hit by his 1981 defeat that his career seemed to be in terminal decline. He was so despondent at having delivered France into the hands of the Left and so aggrieved at what, in an unguarded moment, he called the Gaullists' 'premeditated treachery' that he withdrew from active political life on a national level. He was much revived following the Centre Right's victory in 1986 and had his political appetite fully restored after Chirac's failure to wrest the presidency from Mitterrand in 1988. He took over the presidency of the UDF in 1988 and led the Centre Right in the 1989 European elections. His re-emergence was not welcomed by Chirac, by younger aspirants to UDF leadership such as Léotard, who tried to keep him as isolated as possible, or by an erstwhile potential successor, the somewhat maverick Barre whose showing in the 1988 presidential election was not particularly convincing. However, Giscard was not slow to rebuild the UDF by making his peace with Barre and the younger 'rénovateurs'. At the same time he promoted the Centre Right coalition for major national elections, while asserting the UDF's independent status both within the French Parliament, in relationship to the new Balladur government's performance, and in the European context, by announcing the UDF's intentions to fight the 1994 European elections under its own colours and not as part of a combined UDF–RPR list as in 1989. The UDF's success in the 1993 parliamentary elections and Giscard's role in the Maastricht referendum success may have allowed him to continue to entertain presidential, prime ministerial or simply ministerial ambitions alongside his activities in the European Parliament and his chairmanship of the Auvergne Regional Council. To most people, however, this was always unreal. It was impossible to believe that a successful campaign for the highest offices could be fought on the grounds of experience or that Giscard would not be seen as yesterday's man. When two colleagues of the stature of François Léotard and, most significantly, Simone Weil could declare that Balladur represented a better prospect for the Centre–Right in the 1995 presidential elections, the writing was on the wall for even Giscard to see. Thus on 7 March 1995 he was obliged to concede on national television that he had no prospects of success and was withdrawing his candidature. He gave his support to the Chirac–Juppé team. There was to be no personal recompense. No office was offered, although Chirac thought it politic to consult him over some appointments and some of those close to Giscard, such as Alain Madelin and Charles Millon, found a place in the new government.

Snubbed by the national electorate and by the new government team, Giscard turned his attention to the mayorship of Clermont-Ferrand, seeking to reassure himself that he still had a regional role to play. Clermont-Ferrand had had a socialist mayor since 1959, the year when the young Giscard had previously stood for this office, only to be beaten and to withdraw after the first round. In 1995 history repeated itself. Even the hopes of Giscard living on politically through his son suffered a set-back, Louis Giscard d'Estaing also failing to win office in the same local elections. Perhaps this is the final snub, even for such a political animal as Giscard.

Bibliography

Bell, D. S. (ed.), *Contemporary French Political Parties*. Croom Helm, 1982.

Borella, F., *Les Partis politiques dans la France d'aujourd'hui* (nouv. éd.). Seuil, 1990.

Bothorel, J., *Un si jeune président*. Grasset, 1995.

Chapsal, J., *La Vie politique sous la Ve République*. PUF, 1981 (3e Partie).

Duhamel, A., *La République giscardienne*. Grasset, 1980.

Frears, J. R., *France in the Giscard Presidency*. Allen and Unwin, 1981.

——, *Parties and Voters in France*. Hurst & Co, 1991.

Giscard d'Estaing, V., *Démocratie française*. Fayard, 1976 (Livre de poche, 1978).

——, *L'Etat de la France*. Fayard, 1981.

——, *Deux Français sur trois*. Fayard, 1984 (Livre de poche, 1985).

——, *Le Pouvoir et la vie* (2 vols.). Cie 12, 1988 and 1991.

Larkin, M., *France since the Popular Front*. Clarendon Press, 1988.

Petitfils, J.-C., *La Démocratie giscardienne*. PUF, 1981.

Rémond, R., *Les Droites en France*. Aubier Montaigne (Coll. 'Historique'), 1982.

Slater, M., 'Political Parties', in J. E. Flower (ed.), *France Today* (7th ed.). Hodder and Stoughton, 1993.

Stevens, A., *The Government and Politics of France*. Macmillan, 1992 (chapters 8 and 9).

Wright, V., *The Government and Politics of France* (3rd edn.). Unwin Hyman, 1989 (chapter 9).

3. Le Front national

C. RODGERS

History and development

One of the most noticeable changes on the French political scene in the ten years up to 1995 was the re-emergence of a strong extreme Right movement in the form of the *Front national* (FN). The presence of the extreme Right is not of course a new phenomenon in France: its existence can be traced back to the French Revolution, when its hostility was turned towards Republican ideas, and its aims were to rehabilitate the monarchy. More recently, between the wars, while other countries witnessed the rise of fascism and totalitarianism, France saw the emergence of nationalist, anti-communist, anti-Semitic leagues, the best known and most violent being *Action française*, led by Charles Maurras. Then during the war the extreme Right found expression in the pro-Nazi traditionalist government of Vichy, presided over by Marshal Pétain, whose slogan was 'Travail, Famille, Patrie'. After Liberation, the collaborationist extreme Right was prosecuted and dismantled. However, it soon flared up again: first in the revival of nationalist movements which aimed at rehabilitating Marshal Pétain, and which later united in the CNI (*Centre des nationaux indépendants*); also in the short-lived but dynamic movement led by Pierre Poujade for the defence of the small trader against the new forms of distribution and heavy taxation, the UDCA (*Union de défense des commerçants et artisans*); and finally in defence of the French Empire, in Indochina, and especially in the bitter opposition to Algerian independence. Some virulent supporters of *l'Algérie française* joined forces in the OAS (*Organisation de l'armée secrète*) which did not shun terrorist action.

Algerian independence, granted in 1962, weakened the extreme Right which lost its main mobilizing theme. In 1965, Jean-Louis Tixier-Vignancourt, the extreme Right candidate who openly opposed de Gaulle – the traitor of *l'Algérie française* – only managed to obtain 5.3 per cent in the presidential election. His campaign was led by a certain Jean-Marie Le Pen. The 1960s and 1970s were lean years for the extreme Right. It did, however, gain the support of the integrist Catholics who refused the reforms of the Second Vatican Council, and who, nostalgic for past values, were attracted by the extreme Right vision.

The extreme Right's lack of electoral appeal made them rethink their position. Two groups emerged. On the one hand, there were the *nationaux*, grouped around Le Pen, who were anti-Gaullist, populist and conservative, heirs of the Poujadist movement and of Tixier-Vignancourt. On the other hand, there were the *nationalistes*, a pro-European student movement, *Jeune Action*, which was xenophobic, anti-Semitic, anti-capitalist and anti-communist. In 1960, *Jeune Action* was split into two groups: FEN (*Fédération des étudiants nationalistes*) and *Occident*. Whereas FEN was more interested in a pseudo-scientific justification of the superiority of the Whites and of pagan western civilization, *Occident* preferred violent action, which led to its dissolution in 1968. In 1969, it was re-formed as *Ordre nouveau*. This in turn was central to the formation of the *Front national*, which was officially founded in October 1972. Jean-Marie Le Pen became its president.

Difficult beginnings

The *Front national* was a confederation which gathered together various groups from the extreme Right (pro-Vichy, neo-fascist, former Poujadist, monarchist, in favour of French Algeria), but within which a tension could be distinguished between the two tendencies mentioned above: the more extreme *nationalistes* and the more moderate *nationaux*.

When at the presidential elections of 1974 Le Pen obtained 0.74 per cent of votes at the first ballot, it was obvious that the *Front national* had failed to make an impact and that it needed to organize itself as a political party. Although the disreputable *Ordre nouveau* left the *Front national*, to the latter's relief, new extremist elements were encouraged to join in an effort to strengthen and develop the party. François Duprat was one of these new recruits; he was an exponent of the revisionist thesis which cast doubt on the extent of Jewish genocide during the Second World War and on the existence of the gas chambers. Under his influence and that of the neo-Nazis of FANE (*Fédération d'action nationale et européenne*), the *Front national* started developing extremist – revisionist, anti-Semitic, neo-Nazi, anti-American, anti-communist – themes.

The *Front national*'s further failure at the parliamentary elections of 1978 forced it once again to reconsider its ideology and strategy. It distanced itself from extremist elements (Duprat's fortuitous death made this change easier) and returned to the more traditional themes of the nationalist Right: the populist, liberal thesis that there is too much state and tax and not enough individual freedom. Its more moderate ideological stance, and its defence of traditional values (policies included abolition of the abortion bill, defence of the family, restoration of the death penalty and support for Catholic schools) enabled it to attract the Catholic fundamentalist element.

At the same time as it tried to gain ideological respectability, the *Front national*, under the influence of Jean-Pierre Stirbois, developed a militant local presence. Also under Stirbois's influence, it started denouncing immigration as the cause of France's decline, linking immigration to unemployment and the breakdown of law and order.

These efforts, however, came too late for the 1981 round of elections. At the presidential elections, Le Pen did not manage to gather the necessary 500 signatures to be a candidate; and at the parliamentary elections, the *Front national* only obtained 0.35 per cent of the vote: only seventy-four candidates could be found. It was only in 1983 that the electoral rise of the *Front national* began.

The electoral rise of the *Front national*

Success first occurred in relatively unimportant by-elections, where the candidates were well-known figures of the *Front national*. In the municipal elections of 1983, Le Pen's list obtained 11.3 per cent in Paris's 20th *Arrondissement*. In municipal by-elections at Dreux, Stirbois's list scored 16.7 per cent at the first ballot. The UDF/RPR accepted a pact with the *Front national* for the second ballot, which secured a victory for their joint list. Then at parliamentary by-elections in the Morbihan region, Le Pen obtained 12 per cent of the vote. From this point on the *Front national* was going to be able to secure for itself around 10 per cent of the vote. Except for 1992 – when its scores at both the regional and departmental elections were good – the

Front national has tended to score less well in local elections as it suffers from an inadequate local presence in spite of its repeated efforts to convince local notables to head its lists or be its candidates. However, the overall low scores at local elections often hide local successes.

The following results show the steady presence of the *Front national:*

1984   European elections: 11 per cent (10 seats);
1985   departmental elections: 8.8 per cent;
1986   parliamentary elections (under proportional representation):
       9.65 per cent (35 seats);
       regional elections: 9.5 per cent (137 seats);
1988   presidential elections (first ballot): 14.4 per cent (Le Pen
       was the candidate);
       general election (first ballot): 9.65 per cent but with the
       change in the electoral method, which is no longer
       proportional, one seat only;
       departmental elections: 5.2 per cent;
1989   municipal elections: 2.17 per cent (the *Front national* is
       able to present candidates in only a minority of towns, 804
       seats);
       European elections: 11.7 per cent (10 seats);
       by-election in Dreux (second ballot) 61.3 per cent for M.-
       F. Stirbois;
1991   by-election in Marseille (departmental): 51 per cent;
1992   departmental elections: 12.18 per cent (1 seat);
       regional elections: 13.6 per cent (239 seats, the *Front
       national* was subsequently present in all regional councils);
1993   parliamentary elections: 12.52 per cent (no seats).
1994   European elections: 10.5 per cent
1995   presidential elections (first ballot): 15 per cent (Le Pen
       candidate)
1995   municipal elections: 657 seats.

In 1994, at the European elections, the *Front national* lost some of its electorate to Philippe de Villiers's list. De Villiers's campaign had several themes in common with the *Front national*'s – such as the defence of moral and family values, the assertion of France's greatness, and a desire to see French independence from Europe; and de Villiers obtained 12.33 per cent of the vote. In the 1995 presidential elections de Villiers's vote only attained 4.75 per cent, compared with Le Pen's 15 per cent, which was the best result in the history of the *Front national*, and the extreme right's best result ever in the Fifth Republic.

The *Front national*'s good results at the local elections in 1995 confirm the party's progress at the local level and prove that grassroots work in the establishment of a party infrastructure is bearing fruit. After the first ballot, the *Front national* was able to maintain its list in eighteen towns of more than 100,000 inhabitants, and found itself holding the balance of power in several towns. It is now present in many local councils, and has won control of three towns: Toulon, Orange and Marignane.

It is now more popular than the Communist party with working-class voters. Increasingly Le Pen's share of the vote is associated with social unease. In 1995, the *Front national*'s campaign was marked by two deaths: a young man from the Comoros Islands was killed by a *Front national* bill-poster in Marseille and a Moroccan died after being thrown into the Seine by a group of skinheads, following a *Front national* march in Paris.

The presidential and municipal elections of 1995 show that the *Front national* has become the third force on the French political scene, and its permanence and success is without precedent in European and French history.

National results iron out sizeable regional discrepancies. A map of the distribution of votes for the *Front national* at the parliamentary elections of 1993 or presidential elections of 1995 (first ballot) shows that the best results were obtained in the south-eastern coastal area (where there is a higher density of *pieds-noirs* and north African immigrants), in the *départements* around Paris, and in the industrial urban areas of the north and east. The *Front national* is less successful in the more rural west or centre.

The *Front national* electorate is difficult to define, as, to a great extent, it attracts protest votes. As a general rule, however, it tends to be urban, masculine, and composed of non-practising Catholics. All age groups are represented, but more especially the young, and all social classes, but especially shopkeepers, artisans, the young unemployed and upper management.

Explanation for the rise of the *Front national*

The rise of the *Front national* and its steady representation on the French political scene cannot be accounted for simply. It has benefited from a combination of factors. At first, political analysts wrote of '*L'effet Le Pen*', and it is true that the personality of its leader accounts for part of the attraction of the party. Whether he attracts or repels French audiences, Le Pen does fascinate them as the television ratings show after his numerous TV appearances. He is an effective speaker, and his supposed appeal to common sense, his apparent plain speaking, his simplistic ideas delivered with conviction, grasp the attention of an audience tired of political discourse. But however charismatic Le Pen may be, and however skilful at attracting media attention, his personality does not provide a sufficient explanation for the rise of the *Front national*.

The party's initial success may have stemmed from the victory of the Left in 1981, and the fear which that victory instilled in some right-wing electors. The lenient legislation towards immigration and liberalization of penal policy also further alienated right-wing electors who radicalized their vote. Furthermore, many electors of the Left coalition, especially Communists, grew rapidly disillusioned with government policy and the unpopular economic measures taken from June 1982 onwards. The *Front national* also benefited from the change in the electoral system in the 1986 legislative elections, which for once had a proportional element, thus enabling the *Front national* to gain official representation in the National Assembly and therefore a more respectable democratic platform.

By 1986 the *Front national* had contrived to give itself the image of a respectable party, by playing down its anti-Semitic, fascist, racist elements, and by enlisting apparently respectable personalities – university teachers, civil servants, professionals and former RPR politicians. The conventional Right has helped it acquire a semblance of legitimacy. The RPR or the UDF have agreed, on several occasions, to associate themselves with the *Front national* for elections, and right-wing leaders – such as Pasqua and Chirac – have gone as far as to take up some of the *Front national*'s themes and have hinted at times at the similarities between some of their concerns in the hope of winning over part of the *Front national* electorate.

There are, in addition, more dangerous reasons for the continuing success of the *Front national*. It exploits a deep malaise in French society which has been occasioned by rapid social changes to which French people, and French politics, find it difficult to adapt. Amongst the major causes of French anxiety are unemployment, breakdown of law and order and immigration. In large urban areas all three factors may lead to a volatile political atmosphere. The French also feel – rightly or wrongly – that their national identity is threatened by invasions from without (Americanization, Europeanization and immigration) or from within (immigrants with their high birth rate and often Islamic culture). Their lukewarm 'yes' to the referendum on Maastricht (50.25 per cent) and their rampant hostility towards non-white immigrants (in 1992, 76 per cent of French people thought that there were too many Arabs in France) are testimonies to this fear.

Part of the problem is that all the structures which used to go some way towards providing answers in the past are no longer trusted. The old moral and Catholic values have been undermined in an increasingly secular society. The major political parties seem to have lost credibility with the French, as each has proved a disappointment when in power. In particular they seem to have failed to address the problems, such as immigration, which are at the heart of French concerns. By contrast Le Pen speaks openly of the causes, real or imaginary, of French anxiety, and seems to offer simple solutions.

The programme of the *Front national*

The two key ideas of the *Front national* are '*la préférence nationale*' and the defence of law and order. The party links the presence of immigrants – non-EU, and especially non-white – with high unemployment in France, suggesting that immigrants take the jobs of French ('*Français de souche*') people. The *Front national* also insinuates that a correlation exists between a high rate of criminality and a high number of immigrants. It likens immigration to an invasion, a threat to the French nation, its identity and culture.

To redress the situation Le Pen proposes to give priority to French people in a number of domains: employment, social security, housing and family benefits. In order to encourage a higher birth rate for French families, he suggests the introduction of a maternity income for French mothers who choose to stay at home to look after their children, and abortion would be made illegal. Immigrants would, of course, be excluded from these proposals.

The *Front national* would enforce very strict measures preventing non-EU immigrants from coming into France, making it difficult for those already in France to stay, and repatriating all illegal immigrants. French nationality would be more difficult to obtain. They would ensure that French culture, history, geography and language are taught at school. The party proposes to fight moral degeneracy, crime, drugs and Aids (which it sees as a symptom of corruption). Police would be reinforced, tough sentences – including the death penalty – would be applied, which would require an increase in the number of prisons in France.

Whereas Le Pen advocates a strengthening of the judicial and penal functions of the State, on the economic front, he promotes a reduction in the role of the State: the public sector must be dismantled, and shares in state companies distributed amongst the heads of French families. The *Front national* sees in private property the key to motivation and to a successful economy. Le Pen also recommends cutting taxes for both companies and individuals. A comparison between the 1984 and the 1993 programmes shows however that the *Front national* has moved away from its former ultra-liberalist position, and has adopted the vaguely Socialist orientation and the overtly anti-capitalist discourse of the pre-war German and Italian Fascist movements. Hence the *Front national* presents itself as the champion of small businesses and farmers in the face of aggressive international companies, of unfair third-world competition and detrimental EU legislation. The *Front national* also claims that its proposals would help poorer French people by, for example, keeping and increasing the value of the SMIC (*salaire minimum interprofessionnel de croissance*) and the RMI (*revenu minimum d'insertion*),[1] and increasing the lowest wages. But a closer look at its programme shows that its implementation would lead to the welfare state being undermined and inequalities increased; its socializing discourse is only a veneer to attract the deprived of French society.

The *Front national* sets its reforms within a republican, democratic framework, overtly defending democratic rules, and complaining of the lack of democracy in the non-proportional-representation methods used for some elections, from which the *Front national*, as a small party, suffers. It denounces the oligarchies of the main political parties ('la bande des quatre': RPR, UDF, PS and PC) and the 'media plot' which, it claims, victimizes it and denies it expression. Trade unions are also stigmatized for their monopolistic representation of the work-force. The *Front national* asserts that it wants to return power to the French people, and to set up a real democracy where the people could express themselves directly through referendums that they could also initiate. Other aspects of the *Front*'s policy are to ensure the defence of the French nation through the promotion

---

[1] SMIC is the guaranteed minimum wage, and RMI is the minimum benefit paid to those with no other source of income.

of a strong army, the reintegration of France within NATO, and adherence to a non-federal Europe.

Beneath the official programme of the *Front national*, which is more an opportunistic mosaic of right-wing ideas from various movements than a well thought-out, coherent programme, simmers an unofficial, murky culture which flares up at times, threatening the appearance of respectability which the *Front national* has been at pains to create. There is the complete lack of democracy within the party which Le Pen rules like a despot; the *Front*'s liking for military-looking demonstrations which often end in violence; the political background of some of the *Front national* leaders or sympathizers – former Nazis, OAS militants and torturers during the Algerian war; and a strong current of racism and anti-Semitism, which normally takes the insidious form of a supposed respect for difference, but which bursts out in openly racist or anti-Semitic remarks. For example, Le Pen in 1987 came out famously with: 'Je suis passionné par l'histoire de la Deuxième guerre mondiale. Je me pose un certain nombre de questions. Je ne dis pas que les chambres à gaz n'ont pas existé. Je n'ai pas pu moi-même en voir. Je n'ai pas étudié spécialement la question. Mais je crois que c'est un point de détail de l'histoire de la Deuxième guerre mondiale.' Similarly in 1988, he made what he claims to be a mere pun on the name of the minister M. Durafour, calling him M. Durafour-crématoire. Are these mistakes revealing of Le Pen's anti-Semitism calculated provocation to attract media attention, or mere blunders? He constantly performs a balancing act between the need to highlight the *Front national*'s difference from the Right, and thus satisfy a hard core of neo-Fascists, and the danger of going too far and thus losing a more moderate wing of electors who vote for the *Front national* mainly to protest against the other parties.

Conclusion

The enduring presence of the *Front national* is a significant phenomenon which cannot be ignored. It has been a thorny partner for the Right which at first found it difficult to know what line to choose – whether to stress its closeness with the *Front national* in the hope of winning over some of its electorate and of defeating the Left, but thus risking the loss of its more centrist members, or to ostracize it, but with the danger that it might lose its more radical elements to that party.

It seems however that even with a favourable proportional representation electoral system, the *Front national* cannot obtain more than 15 per cent of votes nationally; this apparent ceiling means that lately the conventional Right has been able to disengage itself from any direct contact with the *Front national*.

The influence of the *Front national* on French party policies, however, is more insidious and cannot be denied: it has certainly forced other main parties from the Right, but also the *Parti socialiste* and the former Socialist governments, to take on board some of the issues raised by the *Front national*, and especially to harden their stance towards immigration. The resurgence of the extreme Right in France has always coincided with periods of uncertainty, and the fact that since 1986 the *Front national* has managed to attract around 10 per cent of the vote is a clear symptom of a deep malaise in French society.

Sources

Text A: Preface by Jean-Marie Le Pen to *L'Alternative nationale, 300 mesures pour la renaissance de la France (Front national, Programme de gouvernement*, 1993), pp. 8–10

Confrontés aux redoutables défis qui se profilent à l'aube du IIIe millénaire, les gouvernants devront choisir: l'indispensable audace des solutions ou l'abandon paresseux à un esprit 'fin de siècle' qui semble tenir pour acquis notre déclin.

Le spectacle monotone que proposent les politiciens en pérorant chaque jour à la télévision montre assez quel choix ils ont déjà fait. Dans l'étalage de la médiocrité ou la complaisance pour l'échec, ils sont indissociables: socialistes et communistes, bien sûr, dont la déroute est patente; mais tout autant RPR et UDF, frères ennemis d'une prétendue opposition qui n'a jamais pu, ni même voulu, s'opposer à rien.

Comment croire qu'ils feront enfin demain ce qu'ils n'ont pas même esquissé hier? Pendant deux décennies, ils ont laissé croître de façon dramatique dans notre pays le chômage, l'insécurité et une immigration massive. Pendant deux décennies, ils ont laissé diminuer votre pouvoir d'achat et s'installer une inquiétude permanente du lendemain pour vous et les vôtres. Pendant deux décennies, ils ont laissé se déliter le tissu social et toute société civilisée que sont la famille, l'enseignement, la justice et la défense nationale. Ils ont continué de dégrader notre environnement et laissé ruiner notre agriculture au nom d'une logique exclusivement quantitativiste et matérialiste.

C'est aussi cet abandon de toute référence morale qui les a conduits, toutes tendances confondues, à accepter avec complaisance et allégresse les pots-de-vin et les financements occultes de leurs campagnes électorales, ou à patauger dans les magouilles et les 'affaires',[1] pour finir éclaboussés dans l'abominable scandale du sang contaminé.[2] **L'Établissement politicien a ôté la parole au peuple pour la confisquer à son seul profit.** Il s'aligne de plus en plus servilement sur des puissances étrangères à l'extérieur et sur des lobbies à l'intérieur et, avec la complicité d'un pouvoir médiatique aux ordres, il bâillonne systématiquement ceux qui s'efforcent de faire entendre la voix de la vérité. En un mot, il a abaissé l'État en France et fait perdre à notre pays son rang dans le monde.

Si vous voulez vraiment que change cet état de choses, ne tolérez plus la domination de ces chevaux de retour de la politique, impuissants et corrompus. Tournez-vous vers d'autres femmes, d'autres hommes, des Français comme vous qui, loin des marigots de la politique politicienne, n'ont trempé dans aucun scandale, n'ont accepté aucune compromission: les femmes et les hommes du Front national. Mains propres et tête haute, ils possèdent le courage des solutions hardies et novatrices et la ferme volonté de les mettre en œuvre avec pugnacité et persévérance. Ils incarnent la seule alternative pour sauver notre pays du processus mortel de la décadence.

Les 300 mesures qu'ils préconisent et que vous allez maintenant découvrir sont le fruit d'un travail d'équipe mené par des commissions de spécialistes, tenant compte des derniers développements de l'actualité et des indices les plus récents. Ces propositions démontrent amplement qu'au seuil de l'an 2000, seul le Front

---

[1] Throughout the 1980s, several shady deals and practices involved not only Socialist ministers but also personalities from the opposition (UDF, RPR) who took advantage of their parliamentary immunity, or their position of power, or made use of inside information. These affairs were blown up by the press and turned into scandals.

[2] This refers to the fact that HIV-contaminated blood went on being used for transfusions for economic reasons long after the dangers were known, with devastating consequences, especially for haemophiliacs. France was rocked by this scandal, especially as three ministers were involved, including the prime minister, Laurent Fabius.

national possède un programme cohérent pour assurer la renaissance de la France et lui rendre son rôle dans le monde.

Homme de foi, je crois avec passion que le déclin n'est pas inéluctable et qu'il y a pour la France un avenir de grandeur et d'espoir, si chacun de nous accepte d'accomplir son devoir de citoyen avec courage et honnêteté.

Text B: *Pour la France, Programme du Front national* (Albatros, 1985), pp. 37–8

(In a rhetorical, interrogative tone, Le Pen sets out the main tenets of the *Front national*'s programme in 1985.)

Recentrer le débat politique et électoral sur les aspirations populaires

Ainsi le débat politique et électoral doit concerner la défense de l'identité nationale et la qualité de la vie des **Français** qui passent aujourd'hui par la maîtrise de l'immigration. Il ne suffit pas de le dire, il faut préciser comment on le fera et répondre à toute une série de questions. Les étrangers en situation clandestine seront-ils ou non expulsés? Et comment? Les chômeurs étrangers présents en France seront-ils reconduits à la frontière ou non? **Le code de la nationalité** qui attribue automatiquement la qualité de Francais à un certain nombre d'étrangers sans contrôle préalable sera-t-il révisé ou non? **Les allocations familiales** dont la finalité démographique est évidente, seront-elles réservées aux Français ou non? La loi instituant **une carte de séjour** et de travail de 10 ans sera-t-elle abrogée ou non?

Le débat politique et électoral doit aussi porter sur l'insécurité et les manières de la maîtriser. Mais il ne suffit pas d'affirmer qu'on veut lutter contre la délinquance, il faut dire comment on le fera. Il faut préciser quels moyens nouveaux seront accordés à la police. Dire si les contrôles préventifs d'identité seront à nouveau utilisés ou non. Préciser les modifications qui seront apportées au **code pénal.** Dire si oui ou non la peine de mort sera rétablie et dans quel délai. Dire si l'on est partisan ou non de peines de prison fermes, y compris pour les petits délinquants. Dire si les individus particulièrement dangereux seront à nouveau enfermés ou non dans des quartiers de haute sécurité (QHS). Dire si les peines prononcées seront effectivement appliquées ou non et si les juges de l'application des peines seront supprimés ou non.

Le débat politique et électoral doit aussi s'intéresser au **désengagement de l'Etat**. Mais il ne suffit pas de 'sauter comme un cabri' en disant 'moins d'Etat, moins d'Etat',[1] il faut préciser quelles sont les entreprises qui seront rendues au **secteur privé** et par quelle procédure. Il faut préciser quels seront les monopoles (postes, EDF) qui seront supprimés. Il faut dire quelles seront les réglementations qui seront supprimées. Le débat politique et électoral doit enfin concerner l'impôt. Il faut dire comment on maîtrisera les dépenses publiques et quelle politique fiscale on suivra. Dans quels délais procédera-t-on à des diminutions d'impôts? Prendra-t-on ou non modèle sur le Président Reagan qui diminua la fiscalité dès son arrivée au pouvoir et sur Margaret Thatcher qui procéda très rapidement à une diminution des taux de l'impôt sur le revenu? Sur tous ces points les électeurs n'attendent pas des promesses vagues mais des engagements précis.

Le Front national les a pris; il les renouvelle dans ce manifeste et il souhaite que les autres partis se prononcent pour que les électeurs soient dûment informés. Il est facile de se prétendre un parti de gouvernement, voire de se réserver cette appellation comme le RPR et l'UDF ont tendance à le faire, encore faut-il être à même de prouver que sur toutes les questions de gouvernement justement on a des solutions et qu'on est prêt à s'engager sur elles. Dans l'opposition, seul le Front national a pris des positions précises sur tous les sujets les plus délicats: emploi, fiscalité, immigration, insécurité.

Text C: *L'Alternative nationale, 300 mesures pour la renaissance de la France (Front national, Programme de gouvernement, 1993), pp. 37, 45–7*

(This text comes from the first chapter of the 1993 programme of the *Front national* which is devoted to the issue of immigration. That the programme begins with immigration reflects the importance of this question for the *Front national*.)

---

[1] During a televised interview in 1965, de Gaulle got up dramatically from his seat, and made the following and now well-known pronouncement against the idea of a federal Europe: 'Bien entendu, on peut sauter sur sa chaise comme un cabri en disant: l'Europe! l'Europe! L'Europe!' While reusing de Gaulle's formula, the text of the *Front national* may also be referring to Giscard d'Estaing's wish to curb the role of the State as described in *La Démocratie française*.

La préférence nationale
Ajoutons que, dans les relations avec l'étranger, le principe de la **préférence nationale** – le Français jouit en France de privilèges auxquels l'étranger ne peut accéder – doit prévaloir. Cette notion, qui ne relève nullement de l'égoïsme, de la frilosité ou d'un refus d'ouverture aux autres, est simplement la conséquence concrète de l'existence de la communauté nationale. En effet, si les étrangers possédaient tous les droits et avantages des Français, où serait la différence entre les nationaux et les autres? Et si aucune différence ne subsistait, que resterait-il de l'existence de la communauté des Français?

Ajoutons que la préférence nationale est en quelque sorte un devoir de fraternité ou de solidarité entre compatriotes comparable aux liens qui unissent les membres d'une même famille. Il s'agit donc en réalité d'une exigence morale liée à l'appartenance à la nation . . .

La préférence nationale: arrêter les pompes aspirantes
Il ne suffit pas de développer une politique stricte de contrôle des frontières. Il faut, parallèlement, dissuader les immigrés du tiers monde de venir en France.

Pour cela, il convient de stopper les pompes aspirantes de l'immigration, c'est-à-dire limiter le versement aux immigrés des avantages sociaux existant en France.

16. Accorder la priorité d'emploi aux Français
[. . .]

17. Assurer aux nationaux la priorité d'accès aux logements sociaux
Le parc HLM[1] français est largement occupé par des familles nombreuses immigrées, alors que les listes d'attente pour l'attribution de ces logements à des Français sont de plus en plus longues.

Les Français et les ressortissants de la CEE doivent donc bénéficier d'une priorité dans l'attribution de logements sociaux et de prêts immobiliers leur permettant de s'en rendre propriétaires. Par ailleurs, les foyers Sonacotra[2] seront progressivement transformés en centres d'hébergement pour les plus nécessiteux de nos compatriotes.

18. Réserver les allocations familiales aux familles françaises
Ainsi que cela était précisé dans leur acte de création, les prestations familiales sont destinées à encourager la natalité et les familles françaises. Elles ne doivent donc pas servir de rentes de situation aux

---

[1] *Habitation à loyer modéré*: the French equivalent of council houses.
[2] These are places which offer accommodation to immigrant workers (around 30,000 beds in France).

familles nombreuses immigrées. Les allocations familiales qui seront par ailleurs inscrites au budget de l'Etat,³ seront exclusivement réservées aux familles françaises et à celles des ressortissants de la Communauté européenne sous réserve de réciprocité.

19. Donner aux Français la priorité d'accès aux aides sociales
L'octroi, parfois même aux clandestins, d'aides sociales de toutes sortes encourage l'arrivée massive de nouveaux immigrés et les dissuadent de repartir vers leurs pays d'origine.

Les clandestins ne recevront plus ces aides qui seront versées aux Français et aux ressortissants de la CEE.

Le RMI⁴ sera réservé aux nationaux et aux ressortissants communautaires, sous réserve de réciprocité.

20. Créer une contribution patronale d'aide au retour des immigrés
Pour donner un caractère concret au principe de la préférence nationale en matière d'emploi et pour faire payer aux employeurs les charges induites par l'immigration (logements, écoles, retour) il sera créé une contribution patronale assise sur le salaire versé aux étrangers. Cette contribution pourra être affectée à l'aide au retour des étrangers chez eux.

Text D: *L'Alternative nationale, 300 mesures pour la renaissance de la France (Front national, Programme de gouvernement, 1993)*, pp. 249–50

EMPLOI, DU TRAVAIL POUR LES FRANÇAIS
DIMINUER LA DEMANDE DE TRAVAIL
5. Assurer aux Français la priorité de l'emploi
Appliquer le principe de la **préférence nationale** est une exigence morale pour la collectivité. La présence d'une très forte population immigrée en pleine période de chômage contribue à aggraver le sous-emploi des **actifs** français. Une politique de plein emploi pour les nationaux conduit donc naturellement à instaurer ce principe dans ce domaine.

Des **dispositions législatives** seront prises visant à rétablir la priorité d'embauche pour les Français et leur maintien prioritaire dans l'entreprise en cas de licenciement.

---

³ At the moment family allowances come from the Sécurité sociale, which is not part of the public sector.
⁴ *Revenu minimum d'insertion*, created in 1988. A sum of money that guarantees a minimum income to the most deprived, on the condition that they make an effort to fit in to society.

Par ailleurs, taxer le travail immigré est une nécessité économique. Les immigrés représentent en effet pour l'ensemble de la collectivité nationale un coût exorbitant estimé pour l'année 1989 à 211 milliards de francs. Il est donc normal que les entreprises qui emploient des immigrés et qui par là contribuent à imposer au pays cette charge payent une **contribution spécifique assise sur la masse salariale des travailleurs étrangers.** Contribution qui sera appliquée à tous les **ressortissants** des pays avec lesquels la France n'aura pas passé d'accords particuliers et concernera l'ensemble des branches, sauf dérogation pour motif économique.

6. Organiser le départ des immigrés pour réduire le nombre des demandeurs d'emploi

Un million d'emplois, aujourd'hui tenus par des immigrés, sont susceptibles d'être pourvus par des Français actuellement au chômage. De même, les statistiques du chômage font état de plusieurs centaines de milliers de chômeurs immigrés indemnisés par les ASSEDIC.[1] Le retour des immigrés dans leur pays d'origine libérera un nombre considérable de postes de travail sur le marché de l'emploi, réduisant d'autant le chômage des Français.

7. L'institution du revenu maternel ou parental libérera des postes de travail

L'instauration du **revenu parental** incitera certains parents et en particulier des femmes actuellement salariées à réorienter leur activité. Celles qui auraient préféré se consacrer à plein temps à l'éducation de leurs enfants mais n'ont pu le faire faute de disposer de ressources suffisantes seront dès lors incitées à quitter leur emploi. Ainsi se trouveront libérés des postes susceptibles d'être occupés par des chômeurs.

Text E: *L'Alternative nationale, 300 mesures pour la renaissance de la France (Front national, Programme de gouvernement,* **1993), pp. 72–4**

La transmission de l'héritage culturel
L'école doit être celle de la nation, car elle a pour mission de transmettre aux nouvelles générations l'héritage culturel de notre civilisation.

---

[1] *Associations pour l'emploi dans l'industrie et le commerce*: unemployment benefit scheme to which employees and employers must contribute.

Il convient, à cet égard, de permettre aux futurs citoyens de se situer dans l'espace et dans le temps. Aussi l'enseignement de l'histoire, de la géographie et de la littérature apparaît-il essentiel et doit donc être renforcé.

Encore faut-il que l'étude de la littérature porte sur les œuvres classiques et non sur les livres de gare, que celle de la géographie soit centrée sur la France et l'Europe, que les cours d'histoire cessent de se réduire aux deux périodes troublées de la Révolution et de la dernière Guerre mondiale. C'est l'ensemble de la mémoire française qui doit être transmise aux jeunes Français en s'appuyant sur la chronologie.

L'effort, le mérite et la morale

L'instruction doit également prendre en compte cette réalité incontournable de l'existence: il n'y a ni formation ni acquisition de connaissances sans travail. L'école devra donc réhabiliter cette notion, admettre le principe de l'émulation et de la **sélection par le mérite**. Et, pour récompenser l'effort et le talent, il conviendra de rétablir les examens, les notations, les classements et les prix, car, en renonçant à cette nécessaire sélection, on supprime certes l'échec scolaire mais pour le retrouver plus tard sous la forme de revers professionnels.

L'école est aussi un lieu d'apprentissage des disciplines sociales. Et, à ce titre, l'instruction civique est à réhabiliter, de même que les cours de morale, à condition naturellement qu'ils ne se transforment pas en séances d'endoctrinement politique. Il convient d'inculquer aux enfants des notions élémentaires et essentielles comme le respect du bien d'autrui et de la propriété publique, l'honnêteté, la propreté, la solidarité, la famille, la patrie.

Text F: *L'Alternative nationale, 300 mesures pour la renaissance de la France (Front National, Programme de gouvernement, 1993), pp. 283–5*

MORALE, RESPONSABILITE ET PEINE[1]

La sécurité: Fondement de la civilisation

La sécurité et la justice constituent les missions premières de l'Etat. C'est à lui que revient la tâche primordiale de faire respecter l'ordre

---

[1] Together with the fight against immigration, the defence of law and order is high on the *Front national*'s agenda. Elsewhere in its programme the *Front national* links immigration and crime: '*L'immigration est donc une source majeure d'insécurité*' and '*proportionnellement, les étrangers commettent plus de crimes et de délits que les Français*' (p. 33).

public et les lois, c'est à lui qu'est conférée la charge de rendre la justice. S'il se dérobe à sa mission, la société risque de basculer dans l'anarchie, tant il est vrai que c'est bien l'état de sécurité et le règne de la justice qui font la différence entre la barbarie et la civilisation. L'Etat doit donc donner à cette tâche une priorité absolue et doter la police et la justice des moyens nécessaires à l'accomplissement de leur mission.

La vraie prévention: la morale

Pour rétablir la sécurité, il convient naturellement d'œuvrer à la prévention des crimes et délits. Mais celle-ci ne doit pas se résumer, comme en régime socialiste, à demander aux contribuables de **financer les vacances des voyous des cités** ou à les faire encadrer par de prétendus éducateurs. La vraie prévention consiste en une grande politique familiale permettant aux parents d'assumer leurs responsabilités vis-à-vis de leurs enfants. Elle passe également par la réforme de l'école, afin que celle-ci œuvre de nouveau à l'apprentissage des disciplines sociales et de la morale civique. Il faut dans tous les domaines, médias compris, réhabiliter la distinction morale entre le bien et le mal.

La vraie dissuasion: la peine

Pour autant, le crime, lorsqu'il a été commis, doit être puni. Et le rétablissement de la sécurité exige que soit restaurée la notion de peine. Car celle-ci a une triple mission: dissuader, empêcher la récidive, faire justice.

S'agissant de la dissuasion, la peine, par la menace qu'elle fait peser, décourage les comportements et les actes délictueux: elle ôte au citoyen l'envie de rompre la paix publique par des manifestations de violence ainsi que de porter atteinte à l'intérêt d'autrui et aux règles de droit.

La peine doit aussi empêcher la réitération des actes délictueux par la neutralisation de son auteur sous la forme d'une détention, ou de façon définitive lorsque la peine capitale lui a été appliquée.

Quant au volume de la délinquance, il dépend du nombre d'individus potentiellement dangereux qui sont en liberté: ce sont les amnisties présidentielles qui, en relaxant des milliers de détenus n'ayant pas fini de purger leur peine, ont provoqué l'explosion de la délinquance en 1981–1982 et en 1988–1989.

La peine a enfin pour fonction de faire justice, c'est-à-dire d'apaiser ou d'atténuer le scandale provoqué par le délit ou le crime, de remettre les choses en ordre sur le plan moral par une réaction appropriée au désordre et, en même temps, de consacrer la responsabilité de l'auteur du désordre et de lui rendre une certaine forme de dignité. '**Justice est faite**': tel est le sens du but rétributif de la peine.

La philosophie de la responsabilité
Encore convient-il de renoncer à la philosophie d'inspiration marxiste qui prévalait hier encore et selon laquelle le coupable ne serait pas responsable puisqu'il ne serait qu'une victime de la société.

C'est une conception plus digne et plus noble de l'homme qui doit être rétablie: tout être humain, en dehors de cas pathologiques exceptionnels, est libre et donc responsable de lui-même et de ses actes. S'il commet un crime, il en est donc responsable et doit être puni en conséquence.

La chaîne de la sanction
Pour convaincre le criminel ou le délinquant potentiel de la certitude de la sanction, il faut renforcer toute la chaîne de la répression. Ainsi les services de police doivent être rendus plus efficaces dans la chasse aux délinquants et aux criminels. Une fois appréhendés, ceux-ci doivent être poursuivis de façon systématique. Reconnus coupables, ils doivent subir une sanction sévère et, une fois condamnés, purger effectivement leur peine.

Il convient donc de limiter les pratiques laxistes qui se sont glissées dans la chaîne policière et judiciaire et réduire le laps de temps qui sépare l'accomplissement de la faute du jugement et de la condamnation. Ainsi la peur quittera-t-elle le camp des honnêtes gens pour retrouver celui des malfaiteurs.

Text G: *L'Alternative nationale, 300 mesures pour la renaissance de la France (Front national, Programme de gouvernement, 1993)*, pp. 360–1

L'Europe de l'insécurité et de l'égoïsme
Les accords de Schengen,[1] le traité de Maastricht[2] participent de la même logique. Ils ne sont nullement des aboutissements, un 'plus'

---

[1] Treaty which aims at abolishing all border controls at the frontiers of the signatories. Its implementation could lead to more immigrants coming in from the East via Germany, especially in France where conditions for immigrants have tended to be more advantageous.

[2] This treaty was signed in 1991 by the heads of state of the twelve member countries of the EEC. It aims at creating an economic and monetary union between the twelve, which implies a single currency and a common foreign policy. The Maastricht Treaty was the subject of a referendum in France in autumn 1992 and the FN campaigned against ratification.

ou un 'mieux' pour la 'construction' européenne, mais de simples étapes, soigneusement découpées, homéopathiquement distillées, qui, au travers du nivellement des identités ('il reste un verrou à faire sauter, et c'est celui de la nation'), mènent à l'utopie du gouvernement mondial.

L'abolition des frontières, l'instauration d'une monnaie unique, le renforcement des pouvoirs de la Commission, le rôle donné au Parlement européen en matière de législation nationale . . ., tout concourt à cet objectif.

L'Europe qu'on nous fabrique est bien celle de notre insécurité: en favorisant une immigration planétaire incontrôlée, elle crée les conditions futures d'une guerre civile, du type de celle qu'elle a encouragée par son aveuglement dans l'ex-Yougoslavie.

Par ailleurs, l'Europe communautaire favorise la constitution d'une euromaffia, dont on dit qu'elle est déjà présente dans une transaction immobilière sur trois sur la Côte d'Azur.

Le refus d'intégrer à la Communauté européenne les pays de l'Europe de l'Est participe de la même idée. Mondialiste et cosmopolite, cette dernière ne veut pas accueillir en son sein des patries renaissantes qui se tournent vers le vieil héritage européen pour panser les terribles blessures que leur ont infligées le communisme et le matérialisme.

Enfin, le désarmement envisagé semble particulièrement dangereux, compte tenu des **menaces du Sud** et des incertitudes persistantes à l'Est.

Questions on the source texts

Text A

1. Explain the meaning of the following expressions:
   - *L'Etablissement politicien a ôté la parole au peuple pour la confisquer à son seul profit.*
   - *Il s'aligne de plus en plus servilement sur des puissances étrangères.*
2. What criticisms is Le Pen making of the preceding governments? In your opinion, are Le Pen's accusations justified?
3. What values is Le Pen putting forward?
4. What feelings in the French people is this text appealing to?
5. Study the rhetoric of the text:

- make a list of all the words that indicate decline and corruption, and those which on the other hand refer to moral probity and rebirth. In what way is Le Pen creating a Manichean vision of society?
- find examples of Le Pen's use of passive verbal forms, or terms expressing passivity, to describe the other parties' actions, and active forms for the *Front national*.
- list the words which belong to the vocabulary of war.
- list the images used. What effect do they create?

Text B

1. Explain the following terms:
   - *Français* (in this text)
   - *le code de la nationalité*
   - *les allocations familiales*
   - *la carte de séjour*
   - *le code pénal*
   - *le désengagement de l'Etat*
   - *le secteur privé*.
2. What measures does the *Front national* want to take to control immigration, and why?
3. List the measures put forward by the *Front national* to improve law and order. What do you think of these measures?
4. What is the *Front national*'s concept of the role of the State in political and economic terms?
5. Explain why the *Front national*'s programme, as set out here, could seem attractive to a part of the French population.
6. Have any of the ideas proposed by the *Front national* in this text been taken up by various French governments since 1986?

Text C

1. Show how the concept of '*préférence nationale*' could lead to apartheid in France.
2. Analyse the spurious logic of the first paragraph.
3. Why does the *Front national* want to reserve child benefit for French families only?
4. Find out what other measures the *Front national* wants to implement to curb immigration.

5. Evaluate the influence that the *Front national*'s xenophobic policies may have had on the immigration policy of the current government.

Text D

1. Give the meaning of these words:
   - *les actifs*
   - *les dispositions législatives*
   - *contribution spécifique assise sur la masse salariale des travailleurs étrangers*
   - *ressortissants.*
2. Explain the meaning of these expressions:
   - *préférence nationale.* What does this mean in the context of this extract? Are there other areas where the *Front national* wants to implement this principle?
   - *le revenu parental.*
3. What measures does the *Front national* want to take to reduce French unemployment? What do you think of these measures?
4. Study the style of this passage:
   - the binary opposition created by the text between immigrants and the French, whereby the first are judged to be responsible for the latter's unemployment.
   - the choice of words which present the *Front national*'s measures as necessary and natural.
   - the shift from parent to woman at the end of the text. What do you think of this?
5. What other measures does the *Front national* propose in its programme to reduce unemployment?

Text E

1. Explain why the *Front national* should want to see the following disciplines reinforced:
   - French history
   - French geography
   - literature
   - morality
   - civic instruction.
   Why might it be reluctant to have the French Revolution and the Second World War studied?
2. What does the stress on *travail, famille, patrie* make you think of?

3. Discuss the sentence '*L'école doit être celle de la nation*'.
4. What do you think of the stress that the *Front national* puts on the principle of '*sélection par le mérite*'. Is hard work the only factor that explains success in education?

Text F

1. Who is ultimately responsible for law and order according to the *Front national*?
2. How does the *Front national* propose to prevent crime?
3. What do you think the *Front national* means by right and wrong?
4. How do prison sentences function according to the *Front national*?
5. The *Front national* launches several attacks on the policies of the Socialist government and president. In your opinion, are they well-founded?
6. Analyse how this text presents itself as a return to old values and popular wisdom. What effect does the incorporation of sentences such as '*financer les vacances des voyous des cités*' or '*Justice est faite*' have?

Text G

1. Why is the *Front national* opposed to the EU born out of the recent treaties? Given the values held by the *Front national*, is this opposition to the EU surprising?
2. Explain '*les menaces du Sud*'.
3. Comment on the role that fear plays in this text.
4. The *Front national* promotes the idea of '*L'Europe des patries*'. What does that mean?

Biography of Jean-Marie Le Pen

Jean-Marie Le Pen was born in Brittany in 1928 of a humble background. His father, a fisherman, died when his boat dragged a mine during the war. Jean-Marie Le Pen, then aged fourteen, became a war orphan. An intelligent pupil, he was however expelled from educational establishments because of his rebellious behaviour.

He went to Paris to study law, and there he soon associated with the extreme Right, first with monarchists, then, in 1949, becoming the president of a right-wing law students' trade union (la Corpo de droit). His night-time activities – heavy drinking followed by bouts of violence – led to several court appearances, and finally to the termination of his presidency by his fellow students. He graduated in law in 1952.

Le Pen volunteered to join the French army in Indo-China, but arrived there two months after the fall of Dien Bien Phu. While working as editor of an army newspaper in Saigon, he heard of Pierre Poujade. Back in France in 1955 he became involved with Poujade's party (UDCA), first recruiting young members, then as an MP (he was still only twenty-eight); but he became disenchanted with Poujade's moderation and distanced himself from him. As soon as the Algerian war started, Le Pen joined the army, and was sent to Suez in a crack paratroop regiment. Once again, he arrived at the time of the cease-fire. Sent to Algiers in the capacity of information officer, he took part in interrogations and has been accused of having practised torture, something he first admitted then denied.

Back in France, he continued his participation in violent encounters, and, at an electoral meeting which finished in a fight, he lost his right eye; this explains why he wore a pirate-like patch on that eye for years, before adopting a more acceptable glass eye.

In spite of repeated attempts, Le Pen failed to get involved in the *pieds-noirs* insurrection in Algiers. In 1962, he lost his parliamentary seat. Forced into political inactivity, the extreme Right being in the doldrums after Algeria's independence, he set up a record company – la SERP. The SERP was soon issuing records glorifying Pétain and Nazism.

Le Pen momentarily ceased his political inactivity to support Tixier-Vignancourt, the extreme-right candidate in the presidential elections of 1965. However, like Poujade, Tixier-Vignancourt soon decided that Le Pen appeared too extremist, with the latter's hatred of Gaullism and his wish to rehabilitate collaborators. In any case, Tixier-Vignancourt's poor result put an end to the movement and to Le Pen's involvement.

Le Pen spent his free time sailing – he is an excellent sailor – drinking, associating with a Pigalle pimp, and studying.

In 1972, Le Pen became the president of the newly created *Front national*, and from then on the history of the party became that of Le Pen. In 1976, Le Pen inherited, in circumstances which have been questioned, a fabulous fortune from Hubert Lambert. In 1984, after twenty-five years of marriage and three daughters, his wife left him, but not without exposing in the press the less endearing qualities of her husband: his violence, his male chauvinism, his acute racism. This public scandal came at a bad time for the leader of the *Front national*, who had become conscious of the need to create an image of respectability for himself and his party. With his new wife's help, Le Pen has actively worked on a new image of respectable bourgeois, devoted husband and father, respecter of law and order, admirer of de Gaulle, even former Resistance fighter from Brittany – although he had to give that line up after protests from true members of the Resistance – friend of coloured people, and good Catholic. But at times the reassuring façade cracks, and the more threatening character that still lurks behind is revealed.

Bibliography

L'Alternative nationale, 300 mesures pour la renaissance de la France, Front national, Programme de gouvernement. Editions Nationales, 1993.

Birenbaum, G., *Le Front national en politique.* Balland, 1992.

Bresson, G. et Christian Lionet, *Le Pen, biographie.* Seuil, 1994.

Buzzi, P., 'Le Front National entre national-populisme et extrêmisme de droite', *Regards sur l'actualité*, mars 1991, pp. 31–43.

Chambraud, A., 'La Voie royale du Front national', *L'Evénement du Jeudi*, 1–7 avril 1993, p. 13.

'Comment combattre le Front national', *Le Nouvel Observateur*, 15–21 juin 1995, pp. 26–32.

Conan, E. and Gilles Gaetner, 'Qui est vraiment Jean-Marie Le Pen', *L'Express*, 12 mars 1992, pp. 52–66.

'Contre le Front national, Pourquoi il faut s'y prendre autrement', *L'Evénement du jeudi*, 22–28 juin 1995, pp. 10–24.

Dhamel, A., 'Le Tribun intempestif', *L'Express*, 10 au 16 février 1984, pp. 62–3.

Dossier Front national: 'Des vérités qui font mal', *L'Evénement du Jeudi*, No. 384, 12–18 mars 1992, pp. 38–67.

Frears, J., *Parties and Voters in France.* Hurst & Co., 1991, pp. 111–23.

Jospin, L., 'La Résurgence de l'extrême droite', in *L'Invention du possible.* Flammarion, 1991, pp. 141–64.

La Lettre de Jean-Marie Le Pen, bimensuel du Front national.

Le Pen, Jean-Marie, *Pour la France* (programme du Front national). Albatros, 1985.

Marcus, J., *The French National Front: The Resistible Rise of Jean-Marie Le Pen*. Macmillan, 1994.

Mayer, N., and Pascal Perrineau (eds.), *Le Front national à découvert*. Presses de la Formation Nationale des Sciences Politiques, 1989.

Noli, J., 'L'Après Le Pen commence', *Le Point*, 17 avril 1993, No. 1074, p. 37.

Petitfils, J. C., *L'Extrême droite en France*. PUF, Collection Que sais-je, 2ème édition, 1988.

Plenet, E. et Alain Rollat, *La République menacée*. Le Monde-Editions, Collection Actualité, 1992.

Stevens, A., *The Government and Politics of France*. Macmillan, 1992.

Wright, V., *The Government and Politics of France* (3rd edn). Unwin Hyman, 1989, pp. 209-14.

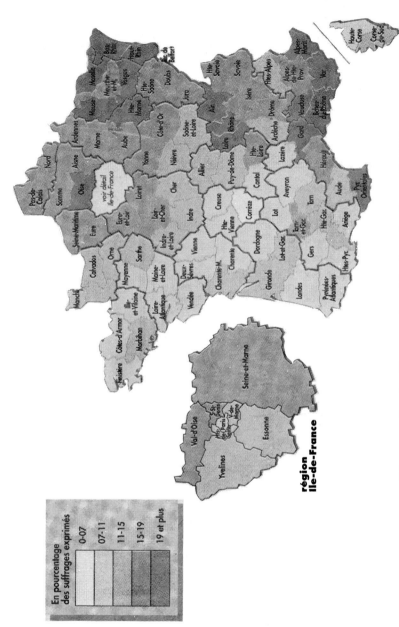

The vote for the *Front national* in the elections of 1995.

4. Le Parti socialiste

N. A. ADDINALL

History and development

The French Socialist party (PS) has a long history going back to the last century which is described by François Mitterrand in the text which follows this section, and in the accompanying notes. Due to its prominent role under the Fourth Republic, it virtually disappeared from the scene with the birth of the Fifth Republic. That it survived in the early years of the Fifth Republic is due in large part to the efforts of Mitterrand, and this period is detailed in his biography (pp. 115–17 below).

The modern party may be described as having gone through three basic phases. The first of these dated from the Congress of Epinay in 1971 (see note 2 to the text by Mitterrand) and shows an attempt to form a union of the Left with the French Communist party, which led to the signing of a Common Programme of Government in June 1972. The failure of the two parties to see eye to eye, however, led to the breakdown of the union and the causes of this failure were attributed by Mitterrand to the Soviet government which, he claims in *Ici et maintenant*, did not wish to see a Communist party in successful alliance with a non-Communist ally, in France or any other European country.

Whether true or not, the situation did not appear to be particularly promising for the Socialist party in the lead-up to the presidential elections of 1981. Without the Communists, where could support be found apart from the Centre which seemed far more likely to vote for Giscard d'Estaing than for Mitterrand? In addition, Mitterrand had suffered two defeats in presidential elections, the last time against Giscard in 1974, when he had already appeared to be the elderly politician whose chances of being elected had gone for ever. Furthermore, the Left had lost the general elections (*élections législatives*) of 1978 and it therefore appeared that Giscard would be re-elected with a clear majority.

Such did not prove to be the case, and this marks the second phase of the *Parti socialiste*'s development. The second ballot saw Mitterrand emerge as a comfortable victor with the somewhat discomfited Giscard now appearing to be *l'homme du passé*. The reasons for his defeat are discussed in the chapter devoted to the *Union pour la démocratie française* (UDF), the General Introduction to Modern French Political Parties in Part II of this book, and by Giscard himself in *Deux Français sur trois*.

From a Socialist party's point of view, one could add that Giscard's defeat was not due only to his mistakes but also, and perhaps more importantly, to the fact that Mitterrand had vastly improved his presidential chances in the campaign leading up to the election by dint of changing his image completely from that of the wily left-wing politician to that of the mature and dignified statesman seeking to represent, as president of the Republic, the interests of all French citizens believing in a decent set of values; in short he targeted Giscard's *deux Français sur trois*.

At the same time, the Socialist party produced – under the influence of its bright new thinkers, Chevènement, Joxe, Jospin and others – a whole host of bright new ideas and solutions for the future to put before the electorate, these being expressed in its programme known as the *110 propositions* and concerning, principally, nationalizations, decentralization, worker-management, and huge improvements in social benefits of all kinds. In contrast with the deflationary measures preached and practised by Giscard's prime minister, Raymond Barre, this programme had much more appeal for voters, particularly young ones; it put forward suggestions for reducing unemployment, reflating the economy, stimulating French industries and considerably improving the financial status of the less well-off. As such it put before the electorate the chance to vote for a bright new future. In addition, the decentralization measures of 1982 (allowing for *Conseils régionaux* to be directly elected and increasing the powers of the region) proved generally popular.

The general elections which followed the presidential elections (Mitterrand having dissolved the *Assemblée nationale* to hold new elections, believing, correctly, that there was now a Socialist majority in the country) saw a comfortable victory for the Socialists. (See election results in Appendix III.)

The period which followed was one of euphoria for the *Parti socialiste* (PS). Although the complete programme was not carried out, large parts of it were, particularly the nationalizations and social measures. The euphoria did not last, however. The results of the reflationary measures were ever-increasing inflation and balance of payments problems, and in 1983 the prime minister, Pierre Mauroy, had to impose deflationary measures and a policy of austerity. He was replaced as prime minister by Laurent Fabius in July 1984.

This marks the beginning of the third phase for the Socialist party, one of economic realism and prudent financial management, which characterized its periods in office from 1983 to 1986, and 1988 to 1993. Opinions within the party are divided as to the significance of this apparent volte-face. Does it mean that the programme should not have been conceived, or if conceived, should never have been applied? It appears that Michel Rocard, in particular, considered that the cost of the nationalizations and social measures, the insufficiently broad base of French industry and the state of the economy in general would inevitably lead to a complete reversal of policies. Others, such as Pierre Mauroy, argued that the austerity measures imposed in 1983 were only accepted by public opinion because of the generosity of the reforms of the previous two years; one cannot expect the population continually to make sacrifices and 'tighten belts' when the end result is not an improvement in living conditions, but the demanding of yet more sacrifices. Whatever the truth of this matter, it can be said that austerity measures are never popular, and it was therefore not surprising that the general elections of 1986 were won fairly comfortably by the RPR/UDF coalition.

The period of *cohabitation* between 1986–8 is discussed in the general introduction to Part II of this book and in the chapter devoted to the RPR. Suffice it to say that the measures taken by Jacques Chirac as prime minister during these two years proved generally unpopular. The privatization of companies which had been nationalized by General de Gaulle himself was not automatically to the pleasing of every Gaullist voter. The attempt to impose selection procedures for university entrance and then to send the riot police to batter students and *lycéens* when they turned out in the streets to protest against them was hardly designed to please either young people or their parents, who were worried not only about the planned cutback in further education but also for their children's safety at the hands of the riot police.

The loss of popularity of Jacques Chirac as a consequence of this was matched by a steady increase in that of François Mitterrand. The very fact that Mitterrand had appointed Chirac as prime minister when he could, admittedly with difficulty, have appointed another member of the new majority, showed him in the light of the true democrat, respecting the wishes of the people. At the same time he was very careful to dissociate himself from the government's policies, on occasion going so far as to refuse to sign government edicts and thereby obliging the prime minister to put the text to the vote before the *Assemblée nationale*. All of this corresponded to the role of the president as defined by the constitution, but Mitterrand also saw how to use the other powers which the president enjoys: in defence matters and foreign affairs he imposed his own point of view, particularly in the latter where at international conferences he was always seen in the forefront with Chirac behind.

The image projected by Mitterrand at the presidential elections of 1988 was therefore a very clear one. He was the cool, calm and capable figure who had represented France at the highest level not only during the years of Socialist rule, but during those of the RPR/UDF as well. He had shown, therefore, how capable he was of filling the role of the arbiter, above party politics, which de Gaulle had set out to create with the institution of the president of the Fifth Republic. By contrast, Chirac appeared to be very much the representative of a political party which, under his prime ministership, had shown itself to be in favour of a Thatcherite, free-enterprise, market-led economy which was far from being popular, even among its own supporters.

The results of the presidential elections of 1988 were therefore, once more, predictable. Chirac's efforts to present himself as the young, dynamic 'go-getter' rolling his sleeves up to 'get on with the job' against the elderly geriatric seemed to have more in common with the image of the football hooligan squaring up to the older, but calmer and more capable referee than anything else. Mitterrand's slogan, 'la force tranquille', seemed entirely fitting, and he won the election quite easily.

As in 1981, he immediately dissolved the *Assemblée nationale* to hold new elections, and was again rewarded by a Socialist majority, but smaller than that of 1981. This time, however, there was no thought of a return to extravagant promises and reflationary measures. The policy would not be one of reversing the Chirac government's measures, but one of 'ni-ni', that is to say, no more privatization, but no more renationalization either. Sound economic policies and a careful management of the mixed economy would henceforth be the path to be followed by the Socialist party under successive prime ministers: Rocard (12 May 1988–15 May 1991), Edith Cresson (15 May 1991–2 April 1992) and Bérégovoy (2 April 1992–31 March 1993).

Following the heavy defeat of the Socialists at the elections of 1993, many people felt that the Socialist party had brought disaster upon its own head by renouncing its principles and following right-wing policies. Certainly, Pierre Bérégovoy must have felt something of this when, as noted elsewhere, he shot himself on 1 May 1993.

Since then, there has been much soul-searching within the Socialist party. On the one hand there are those who feel that it needs to rediscover its left-wing roots and identity and who are not averse to seeking to re-establish a close relationship, and even alliance, with the Communist party, particularly after the creditable performance of Robert Hue, the party's candidate, in the presidential elections of 1995. These are the inheritors of those socialists who, as Mitterrand explains in Source Text A, firmly believed in 'la rupture du système économique, la transformation des rapports de production, l'appréhension par la collectivité nationale des grands moyens de production et de crédit'. It must be said that this variety of socialism, described by Mitterrand as 'historic', has hardly been popular during the 1980s and 1990s, particularly in view of the demise of communism.

Modern socialism has much more in common with the other type described by Mitterrand in Source Text A as 'décentralisateur', 'associatif' and 'partisan des pouvoirs éclatés et d'esprit libertaire'. In spite of the fact that his intention in this text was to demonstrate that there was room within the party for both of these almost contradictory attitudes, it is nevertheless clear from Source Text B where his sympathies lie: 'autogestion', 'décentralisation', 'relations du Plan et du marché', 'respect intransigeant des droits de l'homme, individuels et collectifs' and the conclusion that 'la réponse finale était dans l'homme' have much more in common with the latter type of socialism than with the former, and they have characterized the Mitterrand years.

This conception of socialism, particularly 'autogestion', owes much to the influence of Michel Rocard as Source Text C serves to demonstrate. As Rocard has freely admitted, his brand of socialism is really akin to what is known as social democracy in other countries and he and many other socialists have made it clear in recent years that this is where they consider that the future lies. Due to this conviction and to his popularity in the party, it was he who was supposed to be the official Socialist candidate for the presidential elections of 1995. This was, however, before the general elections of

1993, for which Rocard had foreseen an opening-up of the Socialist party towards the centre and the creation, therefore, of a large new central grouping. The total failure of the party at the elections caused the demise of Rocard and considerable soul-searching as to the causes of failure and where the future lay. If it did not lie in the direction of social democracy, could it only lie in a return to Marxist-Leninist communism? Or was the Socialist party destined to follow the path of the Communist party into oblivion? Such pessimism was surely not justified, however. The Socialist party acquired a new leader in 1995 in Lionel Jospin, and his very creditable performance in only losing narrowly to Chirac in the second ballot of the presidential elections of that year showed that support for the Socialist party was still very much present.

The 'municipal' elections of May 1995 were also most encouraging for the Socialist party. The expectation that, after Chirac's success, the RPR would carry all before it, proved to be without foundation. Although the greatest gains in these elections were made by the *Front national* and the Socialist party lost control of a few towns, it nevertheless performed much better than expected, gaining control of such large towns as Tours, Sarcelles, Rouen and Grenoble and a number of *arrondissements* in Paris and Lyon. That support will no doubt continue for the party which, above all others, considers that it best represents the basic rights of man, as set out by the Revolutionaries in the Declaration of 1789.

Sources

Text A: François Mitterrand, *Ici et maintenant* (Librairie Arthème Fayard, 1980), pp. 19–23

– Rangez-vous la thèse des deux cultures, c'est-à-dire le vieux débat entre Jaurès et Guesde,[1] l'opposition entre les **socialistes individua-**

---

[1] Jean Jaurès (1859–1914) was the leader of the moderate element within the grouping of Socialist parties in 1905 which adopted the name of the *Section française de l'internationale ouvrière* (SFIO). Jaurès was assassinated by a right-wing fanatic, Raoul Villain, for his pacifist views shortly before the outbreak of the First World War. The party split into two at the Congress of Tours in 1920, the disciples of Jaurès continuing the moderate line of trying to reform capitalism from within, believing in decentralization and the freedom of the individual, whilst the majority group, devoted to reforming society through class warfare and State control, became the Communist party (*Parti communiste*). The recognized leader of this group was the long-time anarchist, then Marxist, theoretician Jules Guesde (1845–1922). The

listes, décentralisateurs et les socialistes pour lesquels tout doit passer par le pouvoir d'Etat, rangez-vous donc cette thèse développée par Michel Rocard à votre congrès de Nantes en 1977 dans cette catégorie des drogues douces et délétères? [F.M.] – Mais non, mais non, tout au contraire. Il s'agit là d'un grand, d'un vrai débat. Y a-t-il ou non opposition fondamentale entre le socialisme historique, structuré par des organisations de masse, pétri par les luttes, attaché à des objectifs tels que la conquête du pouvoir d'Etat, **la rupture du système économique**, la transformation des rapports de production, **l'appréhension par la collectivité nationale des grands moyens de production et de crédit**, et l'autre socialisme, que j'appellerai **associatif**, aussi ancien que le premier, mais plus sensible au développement des solidarités de base, partisan des **pouvoirs éclatés** et d'esprit libertaire? A l'écoute de Michel Rocard, à Nantes, on l'aurait cru. J'ai approuvé qu'une telle discussion fût lancée. Je n'ai pas approuvé le caractère tranché et finalement simpliste, qu'elle a pris par la suite comme si n'existaient pas de multiples passages d'un socialisme à l'autre, comme si la synthèse n'avait pas déjà été tentée, et, selon moi, réussie par le Parti socialiste d'Epinay.[2] On ne prouve rien par la caricature, fût-elle ressemblante. Le socialisme historique parce qu'il était marqué par l'empreinte de Marx, a été assimilé, identifié aux vieillissements du marxisme, y compris au travers du prisme léniniste. Puissamment aidé par la propagande bourgeoise qui aurait eu bien tort de n'en pas faire ses choux-gras, le courant sans frontières qui tente d'inhiber le Parti socialiste s'est rassemblé autour de l'étendard, *nouveau Labarum*[3] annonçant 'le socialisme est mort', façon de dire pour être juste: 'leur socialisme est mort', 'leur' socialisme, le nôtre, celui de la lutte des classes et du pouvoir d'Etat, du plan préféré au marché, de la nationalisation des monopoles privés, des revendications de la base. On s'enchantait du syllogisme répandu dans les salons

---

questioner is suggesting to Mitterrand that it is still the case today that Socialists belong to one of these two categories.

[2] The SFIO having changed its name to the *Parti socialiste* in 1969, it merged with the party of François Mitterrand, the *Convention des institutions républicaines*, at the Congress of Epinay in 1971, on a programme of unity, to form the modern *Parti socialiste*. Mitterrand was appointed general secretary, in which post he was to remain for the next ten years.

[3] The *Labarum* was Emperor Constantine's standard embroidered with the cross and monogram of Christ.

parisiens, 'Lénine était dans Marx et Staline dans Lénine, donc le goulag sort de chez Marx.'[4] On oubliait que Jaurès pratiquait **la dialectique marxiste**, Blum aussi,[5] oubli commode pour n'avoir pas à poser la question: 'Le goulag sort-il de Jaurès?' Pourtant, comme dans toute critique, sous les reproches sectaires ou de simple dépit perçait une vérité. **Le socialisme de pouvoir** éloigné du pouvoir empruntait les chemins de son rival en utopie, s'inventait à son tour un monde irréel peuplé d'hommes irréels, ajustait des mécanismes dans le vide et, parti d'une explication scientifique de l'histoire, débouchait, après un long voyage, sur la planète lisse de **l'idée platonicienne**. Et tout cela au nom de la rigueur des faits. On s'était battus pour que l'homme esclave put conquérir sa liberté. On l'enfermait déjà dans la pièce des machines, le cerveau-robot ordonnant à sa place les conditions de son bonheur. Une certaine paresse d'esprit rendue possible par la substitution d'une mystique aux exigences de la raison et à la connaissance de la nature humaine conduisit à ériger en dogmes l'humble démarche de ceux qui cherchent. J'ai dit combien j'admirais les progrès de la science économique et de la science sociale dus aux premiers théoriciens du socialisme scientifique. Ils m'ont convaincu qu'ils détenaient l'explication majeure des temps présents. Mais je me méfie de leur postérité qu'émerveille **la finalité de la ruche**. 'L'homme fait sa propre histoire' disait Marx. Il était sain qu'un coup de vent fît tomber de notre arbre les feuilles mortes de **l'économisme**.

L'autre socialisme, mélange paradoxal de Fourier[6] gratiné de

---

4 Vladimir Ilyich Lenin (1870–1924) was one of the most famous Communist theoreticians, a believer in the dictatorship of the proletariat and developer of the theories of Karl Marx (1818–83). Joseph Stalin (1879–1953) ruled the USSR with a rod of iron through his control of the Communist party and the State apparatus until his death from a brain haemorrhage (assassination was suspected) in 1953.

5 Léon Blum (1872–1950) was a leading French Socialist politician, particuarly influential in the 1930s when he was prime minister of the left-wing *Front populaire* governments in 1936–7 and in 1938. He was also very briefly prime minister under the Fourth Republic from December 1946 to January 1947.

6 Charles Fourier (1772–1837) was one of the early nineteenth-century thinkers collectively known as Utopian Socialists.

Proudhon[7] et corrigé par les Pères de l'Eglise[8] a de l'homme et du travail une idée plus morale qu'économique, se fie au spontané, se méfie des structures dont il redoute qu'elles étouffent plus qu'elles n'encouragent l'initiative individuelle, et, paradoxe encore, faute de croire à sa capacité de transformer la société capitaliste par ce biais retourne au saint-simonisme du père Enfantin[9] féru de modernisme organisationnel. Je le rejoins quand je le vois protéger l'homme, fragile produit du quotidien et de l'espérance éternelle. Je m'en éloigne quand je le vois camper au pied de la forteresse ennemie et se contenter d'emboucher la trompette, comme si les murs allaient tomber, la septième fois.[10] Ces deux histoires ont engendré deux cultures différentes et, il faut l'admettre, concurrentes. J'aimerais mieux qu'elles se complètent pour se fondre plutôt que de s'opposer pour se détruire. Le socialisme a besoin de tous ceux qui rejettent le pouvoir de la classe dominante et refusent l'aliénation de l'homme. Quant à se garantir contre les démons et les vices que tout pouvoir porte en lui-même, les quinze thèses sur **l'autogestion** que nous avons adoptées en 1975 fixent au socialisme sa mission nouvelle: inventer les contre pouvoirs.

---

[7] Pierre-Joseph Proudhon (1809–65), a famous nineteenth-century Socialist thinker, was bitterly opposed to Marx and Communist ideals in general. He was a great believer in humanitarianism and in the freedom of the individual coming before equality. It could be said that the 'socialistes individualistes, décentralisateurs' discussed by Mitterrand in this passage, and particularly Michel Rocard, are his spiritual heirs.

[8] A reference to the prominent Christian element in the Socialist party, and more particularly no doubt, to such prominent nineteenth-century left-wing Catholics as Lamennais, Montalembert, Lacordaire, and to Sangnier who is mentioned elsewhere in *Ici et maintenant* by Mitterrand.

[9] Claude Henri de Rouvroy, Comte de Saint-Simon (1760–1825) is often included in the group of Utopian Socialists, but in fact believed in a mixed economy in which the State and private industry could play complementary roles. He also believed that the Catholic Church had a major role to play in promoting the improvement of the lot of the poorest class in society. Père Enfantin (Prosper Barthélemy) (1796–1864) was, with Saint-Amand Bazard (1791–1832), one of the major propagators of Saint-Simon's ideas.

[10] An obvious reference to the walls of Jericho. Mitterrand is apparently not impressed by what he sees as a mish-mash of utopian and semi-religious ideas.

– Vous avez été deux fois candidat unique de la Gauche, vous avez été le rassembleur des socialistes, le Parti d'Epinay a marqué un grand changement dans la vie politique française. Ce que l'on appelle la Gauche non communiste, brusquement, marchait presque d'un même pas . . .

[F.M.] – Evitons de peindre en rose la situation de 1971. Je ne l'ai emporté que de justesse à Epinay et la nouvelle équipe dirigeante a dû travailler dur de 1971 à 1974 pour parvenir au point où nous en sommes. Il faut dire aussi qu'avant nous Alain Savary[11] avait ouvert notre chemin. C'est vrai que les années 1974 à 1977 ont représenté pour le Parti socialiste un formidable bond en avant et que cette renaissance a pris un aspect légendaire. Mais pour imposer – démocratiquement – la conviction à laquelle adhéraient avec moi une poignée d'hommes et de femmes que j'appellerai l'équipe première, conduite par Pierre Mauroy[12] et composée de douze membres du secrétariat national du début, de nos collaborateurs immédiats et de mes plus proches compagnons, sans oublier le rôle discret et décisif de Gaston Defferre,[13] cela n'a pas été si simple. La nature de notre dialogue m'amène à m'exprimer à la première personne, à employer le mot 'je'. Mais rien n'eût abouti sans les idées, les conseils, le travail et l'amitié de l'équipe en question vite enrichie par des apports nouveaux.

– Je vois bien cet aspect légendaire dont vous parlez: en fait, vous étiez l'homme, jusqu'en 1977 à qui tout réussissait. Je veux dire que votre démarche politique qui partait en 1965 d'une Gauche désunie, d'un Parti socialiste presque liquidé, avec ce score dérisoire de 5% pour son candidat en 1969, avait abouti à faire un grand parti dans une gauche unie.

[F.M.] – Pourquoi parlez-vous au passé?

– Cela marche moins bien maintenant.

[F.M.] – Non, cela ne marche pas moins bien. C'est simplement plus difficile. En passant de 10 à 23, 24% des suffrages, nous nous

---

[11] Alain Savary (1918–88) was a prominent Socialist and first secretary of the new *Parti socialiste* from 1969 to 1971.

[12] Pierre Mauroy (1928–) is the left-of-centre Socialist mayor of Lille, a past secretary of the *Parti socialiste*, and he was prime minister from 1981 to 1984.

[13] Gaston Defferre (1910–86) was one of the most famous Socialists; he held many governmental posts during the Fourth Republic and was a candidate at the presidential elections of 1969.

sommes rapprochés **des zones moins compressibles de l'opinion française.** Après avoir récupéré notre propre terrain, nous entrons maintenant sur le territoire des autres et avançons plus lentement. Normal, non? Le pourcentage que nous avons obtenu en 1978 en dépit de l'échec de la Gauche a été le plus élevé qu'un Parti socialiste eût jamais atteint dans des élections législatives, fût-ce au temps de Jaurès et de Blum. Quant aux difficultés de l'union, j'avais analysé dès 1971, avec mes amis, la contradiction que recélait notre démarche, contradiction inévitable.

– Quelle contradiction?

[F.M.] – Pour que la Gauche pût l'emporter en France il fallait que le Parti socialiste devînt d'abord majoritaire à gauche.

Text B: François Mitterrand, *Ici et maintenant* (Librairie Arthème Fayard, 1980), pp. 44–5

– On reproche au Parti d'Epinay de n'avoir pas su s'inventer un langage.

[F.M.] – Je me suis souvent plaint d'entendre les socialistes s'exprimer dans le langage des autres et subir la fascination de la phraséologie communiste. On m'objectera que cette confusion résulte d'une commune origine, mais cette explication ne me satisfait pas. D'abord le Parti socialiste, bien qu'il accorde une grande importance aux théories de Marx, n'est pas un parti marxiste. Quant au Parti communiste, il est plus proche de Lénine que de Marx. L'âpre rivalité qui a opposé les socialistes utopistes aux socialistes scientifiques, les fouriéristes aux proudhoniens, les marxistes aux coopérateurs, les chrétiens aux rationalistes, avait abouti au XIX siècle à un remarquable épanouissement idéologique. La révolution de 1917,[1] suivie de la dispersion des socialistes en Occident et de leur anéantissement à l'Est a, au lendemain de la deuxième guerre mondiale, provoqué un affaissement de la pensée, un affadissement du langage, tandis que le bloc communiste affirmait, lui, sa cohérence autour d'un pays phare, maître d'une partie du monde, doté des prestiges de la puissance, l'URSS.

De cette expérience soviétique, on mesure aujourd'hui les tragiques limites. Mais le martèlement communiste, soutenu par une presse vivante et nombreuse, par une propagande colossale, par une étonnante maîtrise dialectique, par un dévouement militant sans

---

[1] Mitterrand is referring to the Russian Revolution of 1917.

bornes, a continué de modeler l'esprit de la majorité de ceux qui refusaient le système capitaliste. Le socialisme, le vrai, celui en lequel nous croyons, ne pouvait survivre qu'à la condition de retourner aux sources tout en s'éveillant aux réalités du temps. Nous avons au Parti socialiste beaucoup réfléchi, beaucoup discuté. Notre théorie du front de classe, nos thèses sur l'autogestion, nos projets de décentralisation, notre méthode de planification, notre approche des relations du Plan et du marché et par-dessus tout, notre volonté de fonder la société socialiste sur le respect intransigeant des **droits de l'homme, individuels et collectifs**, nos vues sur la paix, l'arbitrage international, la sécurité collective et le désarmement, notre souci de préserver les équilibres naturels face à la récente mais écrasante domination de l'homme sur ce qui l'entoure, tout cela nous a conduits à l'idée simple, très simple, mais souveraine, que la réponse finale était dans l'homme. Et que cette réponse justifiait notre action.

Text C: From Michel Rocard, *Un pays comme le nôtre* (Editions du Seuil, November 1989), pp. 51–8

L'heure du socialisme démocratique
    Nous vivons actuellement un moment particulièrement crucial de l'histoire du monde.
    Et, comme souvent, lorsqu'une accélération se produit, les espoirs et les craintes se mêlent.
    Les évolutions que connaît le monde communiste, les unes dramatiques, en Chine, les autres prometteuses, en Pologne, en Hongrie, en URSS peut-être, traduisent l'impasse dans laquelle se trouvent des régimes qui n'ont pas su faire toute sa place à la liberté.[1] Les réformes économiques sans la démocratie sont insuffisantes et créent des contradictions redoutables.
    Les réformes politiques sans l'efficacité économique sont toujours fragilisées.
    Les socialistes démocrates que nous sommes peuvent évidemment tirer quelques satisfactions de voir valider par l'histoire les choix faits par les générations antérieures. Mais, ils ont surtout des responsabilités!
    En effet, l'effondrement du modèle soviétique d'organisation

---

[1] A reference to the events which, in the 1980s and 1990s, brought about the demise of the Communist party and the introduction of free elections in the countries indicated, with the exception of China.

sociale nous fait une obligation d'offrir au monde des références et de mettre en œuvre des politiques qui aient une valeur suffisamment universelle pour être une alternative à l'abandon aux forces du capitalisme qui, par elles-mêmes, ne peuvent que creuser les inégalités entre les pays et à l'intérieur de chaque pays.

Nous sommes à un moment où nous pourrions peut-être sortir des confrontations où nous a plongés le grand mouvement de la décolonisation, surgissant dans un monde déjà déchiré par le conflit Est-Ouest. On négocie presque partout. Le désarmement n'est plus un mot tout à fait vide de sens. Des solutions s'esquissent pour lever le fardeau de la dette qui pèse sur le Tiers Monde. Les dictatures sont moins nombreuses.

Mais les incertitudes sont tout aussi réelles. Les différentes situations peuvent encore tourner de bien des manières. M. Gorbatchev[2] peut échouer. **Un conservatisme nationaliste** pourrait alors l'emporter. Plusieurs pays du Tiers Monde sont menacés dans leur équilibre interne. De nouveaux conflits peuvent surgir. La croissance mondiale n'est pas assez assurée. Le chômage, les mouvements migratoires, les contraintes budgétaires sont toujours autant de problèmes.

Face à cela, les points de repères manquent. Les opinions occidentales ont vécu l'érosion des 'valeurs absolues'.

Le scepticisme a marqué des points. Dans des sociétés de plus en plus privées de leurs ciments traditionnels, **la mobilisation collective** n'est pas une évidence.

Or, le socialisme démocratique a rompu avec la dimension messianique que portait le socialisme des origines. L'utopie de la société parfaite s'est trop souvent avérée destructrice.

Nous n'avons plus de programme de transformation sociale clefs en main à offrir au reste du monde! Nous avons abandonné **la vulgate marxiste**, ce n'est pas pour épouser la mode du **libéralisme économique**! Nous continuons de penser que la société peut être

---

[2] Mikhail Gorbatchev [Gorbachev] (1931–) was general secretary of the Soviet Communist party from 1985 and president of the Praesidium of the Supreme Soviet in 1988; he is the man who was responsible for introducing the political and economic reforms (known as *perestroika*) which transformed the USSR. He was elected president of the USSR, and awarded the Nobel prize for peace, in 1990, but subsequently lost his position of power and now is little heard of. Michel Rocard is writing here before *perestroika* has been achieved and his comment that 'M. Gorbatchev peut échouer' refers to the possibility of a Communist backlash, and return to power.

connue et consciemment transformée, conformément aux valeurs et à la raison. Nous offrons une démarche faite d'intelligence du politique, de courage et de ténacité au service de la démocratie, des droits de l'homme, de la protection des faibles. La passion est alors moins facile à soulever! Mais je pense que ce que le socialisme démocratique peut proposer correspond aux nécessités de l'heure et aux attentes du peuple. Encore faut-il être sûr de nous-mêmes, de nos valeurs fondamentales et de notre doctrine! Encore faut-il prendre au sérieux nos valeurs et notre doctrine.

L'Internationale socialiste[3] (regroupement de 77 partis, dont la moitié appartiennent au Tiers Monde) a longtemps dû se situer au niveau des principes. Et elle a représenté alors une référence morale précieuse. D'étapes en étapes, elle a su toutefois renforcer son homogénéité, sa manière d'appréhender les problèmes. Aujourd'hui, je pense qu'il faut franchir une nouvelle étape. Il nous faut déterminer avec force ce que nous sommes et définir les quelques points essentiels qui, comme le levier d'Archimède, nous permettront de proposer au monde les règles dont il a tant besoin.

Je voudrais particulièrement insister sur cette question de l'identité. Mes responsabilités gouvernementales ont plutôt conforté les convictions qui étaient auparavant les miennes et que j'ai présentées au fil des congrès de l'Internationale. Mais, aujourd'hui, je sens particulièrement la nécessité de redire d'où nous venons et où nous allons. Les militants, tout simplement nos concitoyens respectifs, ont besoin de se représenter leur société, ses enjeux, ses devenirs possibles, son avenir souhaitable.

Nous pouvons comprendre les difficultés et les interrogations des partis, des peuples qui doivent aujourd'hui réussir, à l'Est comme au Sud, leur transition vers la démocratie. Nous-mêmes, nous sommes les héritiers d'une longue histoire conflictuelle qui n'a vu se mettre en place que progressivement les éléments du socialisme démocratique tel que nous le concevons aujourd'hui, qui, pour l'essentiel, allie le respect des droits de l'homme, **le pluralisme** et un haut niveau de **protection sociale**.

---

[3] Reconstituted in 1951 at the Congress of Frankfurt, the Socialist International has met regularly on a normally two- or three-year basis ever since. M. Rocard wishes to show here how its numbers have been increasing constantly throughout the world, leading him onto his final argument in this passage about Socialism being 'une bataille pour l'organisation de la planète'.

Pour ce faire, chacun, à un moment ou à un autre, nous avons vu opérer une double dissociation, d'abord celle du socialisme et de la violence, ensuite celle du socialisme et de **l'Etat tutélaire**.

Encore dans les premières décennies du xxe siècle, la culture politique du socialisme démocratique se caractérisait par un double attachement à la démocratie d'un côté, à la révolution de l'autre. Il n'y avait là nulle schizophrénie! Mais seulement la certitude que tout était compatible. La confrontation avec la révolution russe, la théorie et la pratique bolcheviques de la violence d'Etat ont cristallisé l'attachement socialiste à la démocratie. Léon Blum, Kautsky, Otto Bauer, Branting,[4] tous les dirigeants importants de l'Internationale socialiste ont vu et dit qu'il y avait là une monstrueuse erreur et que ce projet ne pouvait aboutir qu'à la violence généralisée, et, entre les crises, à **l'arbitraire**. Les socialistes se sont débarrassés ainsi de la mythologie de la violence. Les socialistes ont pu commencer de mettre en œuvre une méthode de changement social par le compromis, en pacifiant les conflits, non pas en les dépolitisant mais en organisant des confrontations dans la démocratie. C'est ce qu'a voulu théoriser Léon Blum, au soir de sa vie, quand il a proposé au parti français de voir le fondement de la politique socialiste non plus dans la lutte de classe mais dans l'action de classe.

Celui-ci n'a pas voulu suivre son vieux leader. Car, pour beaucoup, il ne pouvait être question de ne plus établir une équivalence entre le socialisme et l'appropriation collective des **moyens de production**.

L'idée de révolution était dissociée de la violence, mais la perspective d'une transformation totale demeurait. Longtemps, les socialistes ont pensé qu'elle se réaliserait par l'élargissement des pouvoirs de l'État dans la redistribution et la production de la richesse. De grands débats sur la socialisation ont longtemps agité nos partis. Il a fallu que chacun fasse son expérience pour associer le choix de la liberté politique à un autre modèle économique. Les Suédois l'ont fait les premiers en 1932. Aujourd'hui, plus personne ne défend réellement une vision étatique du socialisme.

---

[4] For Léon Blum (1872–1950), see note 5 on the passage from *Ici et maintenant* by François Mitterrand. Karl Kautsky (1854–1938) was a Marxist politician of Austrian origin, secretary to Engels and editor of *Die Neue Zeit*, a prominent Socialist paper. Otto Bauer (1881–1931) was one of the leaders of the Austrian Social Democratic party. Hjalmar Branting (1860–1925) was a Swedish Socialist who was three times prime minister between 1920 and 1925, and was given the Nobel prize for peace in 1921.

Evidemment, les controverses ne sont pas près de s'éteindre et il y a bien des manières de comprendre **l'économie mixte**. Mais, sur l'essentiel, nous nous retrouvons pour penser que, si le socialisme demeura toujours un combat pour la justice sociale, il doit se donner la liberté pour règle et la raison comme moyen.

La compétition a des vertus. Mais elle exige des règles du jeu sans lesquelles s'imposerait toujours la règle du plus fort qui est tout à la fois injuste et stupide.

Mais parler de règle du jeu, c'est aussitôt poser la question de savoir qui peut les édicter. La réponse est évidente: il s'agit de la puissance publique démocratiquement conférée. Et c'est ainsi, selon moi, que se pose le problème de l'Etat.

Au commencement sont les droits de l'homme,[5] c'est là une donnée intangible, non négociable, exigeante et, j'ajouterai, efficace. La démocratie n'est pas un luxe: elle est la condition du développement et on ne connaît pas de dictature qui soit économiquement performante dans la durée. Il y a là un constat essentiel pour nos amis du Tiers Monde.

Ensuite, vient l'organisation constitutionnelle et l'expérience démontre qu'il n'y en a qu'une qui vaille: le régime parlementaire rationalisé quelles qu'en soient les nuances. Lui seul peut allier souplesse et efficacité. Le régime présidentiel est un mauvais produit d'exportation. Seules les traditions américaines, et certaines particularités, lui permettent de fonctionner aux Etats-Unis et toutes les tentatives faites pour l'imposer ailleurs se sont traduites par des désastres.

Les droits de l'homme, **le parlementarisme rationalisé**, j'ajoute encore la décentralisation. Il n'est pas de croissance durable sans **décentralisation** du commandement et autonomie des entreprises. Toutes nos valeurs communes sont un pari sur l'homme: celui selon lequel il est doué de raison et apte à être raisonnable.

Encore faut-il qu'il puisse exercer cette responsabilité, agir sur ce qui l'entoure. La puissance publique trouve là son rôle, essentiellement pour lutter contre la violence et les formes d'oppression, pour prévenir les déséquilibres plutôt que d'attendre que le marché les produise, pour préparer l'avenir, déterminer les priorités qui ne peuvent être assumées que par une forte volonté collective.

---

[5] Rocard is presumably referring here to the rights of man as detailed in the *Déclaration universelle des droits de l'homme* adopted in Paris on 10 December 1948.

Nous définissons ainsi un modèle politique de développement et de vie qui allie la liberté, le pluralisme, la solidarité. Il est évidemment perfectible . . . A partir d'horizons différents, trois grandes critiques nous sont parfois faites. Notre projet ne serait plus socialiste. De toute manière, il ne serait pas efficace. Enfin, il ne concernerait que les pays occidentaux. Je voudrais consacrer un court moment à réfuter ces accusations. Car si nous avons été longtemps modestes, le temps est venu de déployer bien haut notre drapeau. Après tout, l'efficacité de notre démarche se mesurera à l'espoir que nous serons ou non capables d'insuffler à tous ceux qui veulent croire, comme le disait Jaurès,[6] à 'la valeur morale de l'histoire'.

Sur le premier point, en fait, notre critique du capitalisme comme système de production marchande n'a pas disparu. Seulement, son angle d'attaque s'est déplacé. Car nous ne souhaitons nullement priver notre société du dynamisme qu'engendre la compétition entre libres entreprises. Nous cherchons seulement à ne pas confondre la justice et le libéralisme économique. Nous corrigeons **la régulation par le marché** non seulement au moyen de l'intervention des pouvoirs publics, mais aussi des syndicats, des associations. Nous entendons, de même, contenir l'expansion indéfinie des rapports marchands, pour préserver un ensemble d'activités, de secteurs, de rapports humains. Pour assurer la cohésion sociale, il importe qu'un minimum d'égalité soit assuré entre les citoyens, tout particulièrement pour l'éducation, la santé, la culture, la communication. Nous n'avons pas renoncé non plus à libérer l'homme dans le travail et dans la vie quotidienne.

Quant au procès en efficacité, que n'a-t-on entendu avec la crise – et qu'entendons-nous encore – tant la mode monétariste marque les esprits! Le socialisme démocratique ne serait qu'un mode de pilotage adapté aux temps calmes de climat économique favorable, quand la croissance permet d'offrir des compensations matérielles immédiates. La crise du keynésianisme[7] signifierait la fin des politiques social-démocrates. Or, que voit-on aujourd'hui? Les pays qui ont le mieux résisté à la crise sont ceux qui ont le mieux préservé leur cohésion

---

[6] Jean Jaurès (1859–1914). See note 1 on the passage from *Ici et maintenant* by François Mitterrand.

[7] John Maynard Keynes (1883–1946) was an economist who believed in State investment and intervention to promote employment.

sociale. La Suède, l'Autriche, l'Allemagne, où le SPD[8] a fait face au plus gros de la crise, et d'autres sont là pour le démontrer. Certes, une politique peut ne pas réussir. Mais partout où, forts de la confiance des salariés, les gouvernements ont pu joindre une politique budgétaire intelligente et **une politique des revenus** jouant sur le temps, ils ont pu limiter le chômage et maintenir un haut niveau de protection sociale. La clef est de savoir et de pouvoir arbitrer entre les profits et les salariés. Enfin, notre modèle ne serait qu'un luxe pour pays riches? Nulle idée ne me paraît plus fausse et plus pernicieuse. Car, enfin, que cherche-t-on dans les pays de l'Est sinon le pluralisme et l'efficacité économique! Que cherche-t-on dans les pays du Tiers Monde sinon plus de démocratie et plus de développement économique? Que cherche-t-on en Amérique latine sinon plus de liberté et plus de protection sociale? Et je pourrais demander en outre ce qu'on recherche en Amérique du Nord sinon un minimum de protection sociale là aussi. En réalité, les éléments fondamentaux du socialisme démocratique, leurs conséquences en matière d'organisation sociale et de rôle de la puissance publique, leurs relations avec le développement économique, social et culturel sous toutes ses formes sont, dans leurs principes, les mêmes pour le Nord et le Sud, pour l'Est et l'Ouest. Les niveaux techniques continuent de fortement différer. Mais la liberté organisée est un principe de développement absolument commun.

Je pense – et je le dis dans forfanterie – que nous avons peu à peu défini ce qui est sans doute le meilleur des systèmes possibles d'organisation sociale et politique pour chaque nation.

Au-delà, je crois également que ce qui est bon pour ces communautés humaines complexes qui se sont progressivement constituées, parfois un peu par hasard, et qu'on appelle les nations, ce qui est bon pour les nations, donc, ne peut pas être mauvais pour l'humanité.

Tous nous savons que pratiquement aucun des grands problèmes ne peut connaître de solution purement nationale.

Les pays sont plus ou moins riches, mais l'économie est une.

Les pays sont plus ou moins propres, mais l'atmosphère terrestre est une.

Les pays vivent plus ou moins en paix, mais aucun ne serait épargné par une guerre planétaire.

---

[8] The German Social Democrat Party.

Malgré cela, malgré l'évidence qui veut que l'humanité tout entière a des intérêts communs, souvent vitaux, ces intérêts n'ont pas de porte-parole, cette humanité n'a pas de volonté et ces questions vitales restent sans réponse.

Lors d'une rencontre internationale récente – c'était à La Haye le 10 mars –, j'ai été frappé par une intervention de notre amie Premier ministre norvégien, Gro Harlem Brundtland. Elle a dit avec vigueur que chacun devait bien comprendre qu'on ne pourrait pas continuer à adopter comme norme de comportement général sur chaque sujet celui du pays faisant preuve de la plus mauvaise volonté.

Le problème est bien là, en effet: sur le plan international nous sommes souvent en quelque sorte condamnés à la bêtise.

Il n'y a pratiquement pas de problèmes sans solution mais pas non plus de solution sans volonté et sans intelligence.

Tout l'avenir de l'humanité se joue donc sur cette question simple et terrible: serons-nous capables ou non de faire entrer l'intelligence et la volonté dans les affaires du monde?

Je l'ignore, mais ce que je sais, c'est, d'une part, qu'il faut essayer, d'autre part qui si ce n'est pas nous, l'Internationale socialiste, qui prenons des initiatives, personne ne le fera.

C'est bien une bataille pour l'organisation de la planète qu'il s'agit d'engager. Organisation de la planète pour la défense de son environnement, organisation de la planète pour redonner ses chances au développement, organisation de la planète pour assurer la paix et ainsi désarmer.

Questions on the source texts

Text A

1. Explain the meaning of the following words or expressions:
    (i)   *décentralisateurs*
    (ii)   *la rupture du système économique*
    (iii) *l'appréhension par la collectivité nationale des grands moyens de production et de crédit*
    (iv)   *associatif*
    (v)   *pouvoirs éclatés*
    (vi)   *la dialectique marxiste*
    (vii) *le socialisme de pouvoir*
    (viii) *l'idée platonicienne*

(ix) *la finalité de la ruche*
(x)   *l'économisme*
(xi) *l'autogestion*
(xii) *[les] zones moins compressibles de l'opinion française.*

2. Explain the meaning of *socialistes individualistes, décentralisateurs* (pp.99–100, l.1).

3. What do you think Mitterrand means by *le socialisme historique?* (p.100, l.7).

4. Explain what may be understood by *de multiples passages d'un socialisme à l'autre* (p.100, 1.18).

5. Discuss what is meant by the *plan préféré au marché* (p.100, 1.29) and the possible reasons for this preference.

6. What happens, according to Mitterrand, when *le socialisme de pouvoir* (p.101, 1.6) is not in power?

7. Explain the meaning of the following sentence: *Une certaine paresse d'esprit rendue possible par la substitution d'une mystique aux exigences de la raison et à la connaissance de la nature humaine conduisit à ériger en dogmes l'humble démarche de ceux qui cherchent* (p.101, ll.15–18).

8. Outline the aspects of *l'autre socialisme* (p.101, 1.26) which are praised by Mitterrand and those aspects which he criticizes.

9. Explain what is meant by *inventer les contre pouvoirs* (p.102, ll.19–20).

10. Give the names of the parties which made up (or still make up) the non-Communist Left.

11. What are the reasons put forward by Mitterrand to explain the slower progress being made by the Socialist party?

Text B

1. What do you understand by *'[les] droits de l'homme, individuels et collectifs'?*

Subjects for further discussion

1. Explain the meaning of Mitterrand's comment that 'pour que la Gauche pût l'emporter en France il fallait que le Parti socialiste devînt d'abord majoritaire à gauche' (Text A, p.104, ll. 11–12). Do you agree?

2. What do you think Mitterrand means by 'la réponse finale était dans l'homme' (Text B, p.105, 1.14)?

Text C

1. Explain the meaning of the following words or expressions:

    (i)   *un conservatisme nationaliste*
    (ii)   *la mobilisation collective*
    (iii) *la vulgate marxiste*
    (iv)   *le libéralisme économique*
    (v)   *le pluralisme*
    (vi)   *la protection sociale*
    (vii) *l'Etat tutélaire*
    (viii) *l'arbitraire*
    (ix)   *des moyens de production*
    (x)   *l'économie mixte*
    (xi)   *le parlementarisme rationalisé*
    (xii) *décentralisation*
    (xiii) *la régulation par le marché*
    (xiv) *une politique des revenus.*

2. Explain what you think Rocard means by: 'Les réformes économiques sans la démocratie sont insuffisantes et créent des contradictions redoutables' (p. 105, ll. 27–9).

3. Since the collapse of communism, the only political alternative to capitalism, according to Rocard, is his brand of 'socialisme démocratique' (p. 106, l. 26). Outline its main objectives, as described in this passage.

4. Rocard claims that capitalist forces 'ne peuvent que creuser les inégalités entre les pays et à l'intérieur de chaque pays' (p. 106, ll. 4–5). Explain what is meant by this.

5. Do you consider that it is a good thing that there should have been an erosion of 'valeurs absolues' in 'les opinions occidentales' (p. 106, ll. 21–2)? If so, why?

6. Give a brief description of what you understand by 'le socialisme des origines' (p. 106, l. 27). What were its main objectives? Have they now been entirely abandoned?

7. What should be the role of the State, according to Rocard? How does he reconcile this role with a belief in freedom and competition?

8. For what reasons does Rocard think that efficient economic performance is not possible without democracy?

9. Discuss the reasons put forward by left-wing critics for not considering Rocard to be a Socialist at all. What answers does he provide?

10. For what reasons is Rocard attacked by right-wing critics? How does he answer these criticisms?

11. Why do some critics consider Rocard's brand of socialism to be suitable only for rich countries? How does he counter these arguments?

12. How does Rocard arrive at his conclusion that the future is about 'une bataille pour l'organisation de la planète' (p. 112, l. 21)?

Subjects for further discussion

1. How far would you agree with Rocard's view that capitalist forces 'ne peuvent que creuser les inégalités'?

2. To what extent do you agree or disagree with Rocard's view of the role of the State?

3. Is it true, in your view, to say that Rocard's brand of socialism is only suitable for rich countries?

4. Do Rocard's ideas appear to you to be utopian?

Biography of François Mitterrand

François Mitterrand was born on 26 October 1916 at Jarnac, in the Charente region of France. His father was initially a French railways official, and later a prosperous vinegar manufacturer. He has three brothers, one a *Polytechnique*-trained engineer, the second a former general in the French air force, the third a farmer and mayor; he also has four sisters. He is married to Danielle Gouze and they have two children.

A graduate with degrees in law, politics and arts, and a higher degree in public law, Mitterrand was only twenty-three and with possible right-wing views when the Second World War broke out and he was conscripted. Wounded and taken prisoner in June 1940, he was to spend the next year and a half in a prisoner-of-war camp in Poland before managing to escape in December 1941 and return to France where he obtained a post with the *Commissariat aux prisonniers de guerre* of the Vichy government. It was not long, however, before he had established contacts with the Resistance and by early 1943 he had become a prominent member of it, operating under the code name of Morland.

He was briefly General de Gaulle's general secretary for prisoners of war in August/September 1944, but his political career really took off in 1946 with the creation of the Fourth Republic.

During its duration he held eleven ministerial posts, although only one of these was amongst the most senior – that of minister of the Interior in Mendès-France's government of 1954–5. It was, no doubt, from these days that the image of him which was prevalent before 1980 as a devious and wily politician derived. This successful ministerial career (if one excepts the fact that he never became prime minister) came to an end with the demise of the Fourth Republic in 1958.

From the beginning of the Fifth Republic onwards Mitterrand saw his role as providing implacable opposition to General de Gaulle. This opposition could only come from the Left and could only be effective if the Left was united. This was the reason why Mitterrand created, in June 1964, the *Convention des institutions républicaines* from a number of smaller Socialist groups. He then negotiated with the Communist and Socialist (SFIO) parties and persuaded them to agree to his proposition to stand as the sole candidate of a unified Left in the presidential elections of 1965.

Although he lost in the second ballot to de Gaulle, it was obvious that the policy of unification of the Left was proving successful. He therefore created a new alliance of the SFIO, the CIR and the Radical party known as the *Fédération de la gauche démocrate et socialiste* (FGDS) in 1965 and sought to arrange electoral alliances with the Communist party.

The *événements de mai* in 1968, however, largely discredited those, principally the Left, who had thought to take advantage of these events to oust the government. In addition, the Soviet invasion of Czechoslovakia, also in 1968, much reduced the popularity of the Communist party. As a result Mitterrand's attempts to create a united Left were temporarily suspended.

They began anew when, as the text from *Ici et maintenant* and the accompanying notes illustrate, the Socialist party and the *Convention des institutions républicaines* merged to create a new *Parti socialiste*, with Mitterrand as its general secretary, at the Congress of Epinay in 1971. The following year saw the signing of the *Programme commun de gouvernement* with the Communist party and it appeared that this time the Union of the Left had been achieved; this impression was greatly reinforced when members of the smaller *Parti socialiste unifié* (PSU), Michel Rocard at their head, also joined the *Parti socialiste* in 1974.

The subsequent breakdown of the Union of the Left is recounted in the History and Development section of this chapter, as is

Mitterrand's triumphal advance to take the presidency of the Republic in 1981 and 1988.

Although his authority was challenged within his own party – Michel Rocard was certainly his main rival in the period after 1978 – it is clear that Mitterrand had the ability to conciliate warring factions and different points of view. The passage reproduced from *Ici et maintenant* illustrates the way in which he held the Socialist party together in spite of the widely different tendencies within it. It also illustrates his anti-communism, which makes his success at achieving an alliance with the Communist party all the more surprising. His successes in 1981 and 1988 also prove that his popularity extended well beyond the parties of the Left. His majority was not that of the Socialist party, it was a veritable *majorité présidentielle*.

It ceased with the end of his second term of office in 1995, and many observers have made the comment that the Socialist party might have been in a stronger position subsequently, and Chirac perhaps not elected president of the Republic, if Mitterrand had not held on to power for so long. Mitterrand himself had written in *Ici et maintenant* that seven years is too long as a presidential term and had added that if seven years is too long, what can be said about fourteen years? When asked by a journalist in 1988 why he was standing for re-election in view of these remarks, he replied that he had changed his mind! Perhaps he should not have done. Successful as he was at holding the Socialist party together, the inescapable conclusion must be that the general public felt – two periods of *cohabitation* notwithstanding – that fourteen years of socialism was enough.

Biography of Michel Rocard

Michel Rochard was born on 23 August 1930 at Courbevoie. Like other prominent politicians, he is a graduate of the *Ecole nationale d'Administration* (ENA). He has four children from two marriages.

He was elected national secretary of the *Parti socialiste unifié* (PSU) in 1967 where he remained until 1973, joining the *Parti socialiste* in the following year. He rose to prominence during the *événements* of May 1968, appearing to be not only one of the most gifted and intelligent voices to represent the student uprising, but also one which was fully attuned – unlike the traditional Left, and particularly the Communist party, which came down heavily on the side of de Gaulle and his government – to the spirit of freedom of the individual which the uprising embodied, as opposed to traditional straightforward Socialist egalitarianism.

He has continued to preach this brand of libertarian socialism from within the Socialist party since 1974, with a very large measure of success. The passages reproduced from his own book, *Un pays comme le nôtre* and from François Mitterrand's *Ici et maintenant*, will enable the reader to understand Rocard's version of socialism. It is a version which has not endeared him to all in the Socialist party and, when coupled to the pragmatic economic policies which he followed during his term as prime minister (12 May 1988–15 May 1991), led a certain number of members of his party to query whether he was a Socialist at all. This dissent does not appear to bother him unduly. He has made it clear that he views himself as a Social Democrat rather than a traditional Socialist, and his views on *autogestion* (much akin to de Gaulle's *participation*, see Part II, chapter 1, on the RPR), ecology, State participation without control, desire to see global solutions to economic problems and overall lack of dogmatism suggest that he is less intent on being at the head of the Socialist party than being at the head of a centre-left coalition.

He has already been a candidate at the presidential elections, gaining 3.61 per cent of the votes cast in 1969. Since joining the Socialist party in 1974 he has risen steadily through the ranks, and has been a minister, prime minister and first secretary of the Socialist party. The results of the 1993 general elections helped to put paid to his chances of being Mitterrand's natural successor, but there can be little doubt that Michel Rocard will play an important role in the political future of the Fifth Republic.

Bibliography

Alexandre, P., *Plaidoyer l'impossible*. Albin Michel, 1994.

Balvet, M., *Le Roman familial de François Mitterrand*. Plon, 1994.

Bell, D. S., and B. Criddle, *The French Socialist Party: Resurgence and Victory*. Oxford University Press, 1988.

Brunet, J.-P., *Histoire du socialisme en France de 1891 à nos jours*. PUF, 1989.

Cadiot, J.-M., *Mitterrand et les communistes*. Ramsay, 1994.

Chevènement, J.-P., *Les Communistes, les Socialistes et les autres*. Aubier Montaigne, 1977.

Colombani, J.-M., *La France sous Mitterrand*. Flammarion, 1992.

——, and J.-Y. Lhomeau, *Le Mariage blanc*. Grasset, 1986.

Daniel, J., *Les Religions d'un Président: regard sur les aventures du Mitterrandisme*. Grasset, 1988.

Duhamel, A., *La République de M. Mitterrand*. Grasset, 1982.

——, *Le 5ᵉ Président*. Gallimard, 1987.

Estier, C. and V. Neiertz, *Véridique histoire d'un septennat peu ordinaire*. Grasset, 1987.

Faux, F., *La Main droite de Dieu*. Seuil, 1994.

Gouze, R., *Mitterrand par Mitterrand*. Le Cherche-midi, 1994.

Krakovitch, R., *Le Pouvoir et la rigueur*. Publisud, 1994.

Manceron, C., B. Pingaud and F. Mitterrand, *François Mitterrand: l'homme, les idées, le programme*. Flammarion, 1981.

Melenchon, J., *Rocard*. Ramsay, 1994.

Mitterrand, F., *Le Coup d'Etat permanent*. Plon, 1964.

——, *L'Abeille et l'architecte*. Flammarion, 1978.

——, *Ici et maintenant*. Fayard, 1980.

——, *La Paille et le grain*. Flammarion, 1981.

——, *Politique*. Fayard, 1981.

——, *Ma part de vérité*. Fayard, 1986.

Moll, G., *François Mitterrand, le roman*. Fand, 1995.

Montaldo, M., *Mitterrand et les 40 voleurs*. Albin-Michel, 1994.

Péan, P., *Une jeunesse française*. Fayard, 1994.

Rocard, M., *Questions à l'Etat socialiste*. Stock, 1972.

——, *Le Marché commun contre l'Europe*. Le Seuil, 1973 (with Bernard Jaumont and Daniel Lenègre).

——, *L'Inflation au cœur*. Gallimard, 1975 (with Jacques Gallus).

——, *Parler vrai*. Le Seuil, 1979.

——, *A l'épreuve des faits*. Le Seuil, 1986.

——, *Un pays comme le nôtre*. Le Seuil, 1989.

Rondeau, D., *Mitterrand et nous*. Grasset, 1994.

Schneider, R., *Les Dernières années*. Seuil, 1994.

Stasse, F., *La Morale de l'histoire*. Seuil, 1994.

There have been many other books published by Socialist politicians such as Pierre Mauroy and Laurent Fabius but the one which most clearly outlines the development of the Socialist party under the Fifth Republic and is also excellent on the other parties is:

Jospin, L., *L'Invention du possible*. Flammarion, 1991.

5. Le Parti communiste français

N. A. ADDINALL

History and development

The French Communist party (PC) came into existence when the French Socialist party split at the Congress of Tours in 1920, the larger group taking the name *Section française de l'Internationale communiste*, the remainder continuing under the label *Section française de l'Internationale ouvrière* which, after its merger with other Socialist groups in 1969, became the *Parti socialiste* (see the chapter devoted to the *Parti socialiste*).

From its beginnings the Communist party has basically followed a Marxist line and taken its lead from Moscow. In its early days this was understandable in the mood of the time as the USSR was viewed by many, particularly amongst the working classes, as a revolutionary new country representing real hope for the future. Its support for the *Cartel des Gauches* in the 1920s and for the *Front populaire* in the 1930s helped to increase its popularity, but it was really in the aftermath of the Second World War that its popularity reached its height, this being due, as mentioned in the general introduction, to the role played by the Communist party in the Resistance, and the general perception that the war had been, at least in part, a victory of communism over fascism.

The elections of October 1945 showed the Communist party to be the largest single party in France and it abandoned its pre-war position of remaining permanently in opposition to provide ministers in the first post-war government of Charles de Gaulle, as well as succeeding governments. The leader of the party, Maurice Thorez, appeared in four governments out of five between 13 November 1945 and 4 May 1947 as minister of state or deputy prime minister, and the ministers for social security, armament, reconstruction and even defence were regularly members of the Communist party during this period. The Ramadier government formed on 22 January 1947 was the last one in which the Communists served under the Fourth Republic; disagreements over the Indo-Chinese War and the Marshall Plan led Ramadier to sack his Communist ministers.

From this point onwards the Communist party remained in opposition during the remainder of the Fourth Republic and much of the Fifth Republic under its successive leaders, Maurice Thorez (who retired as general secretary in May 1964), Waldeck-Rochet (retired 1972) and Georges Marchais (retired 1994). Although in opposition, it did not show itself to be particularly virulent, particularly during the *événements* of 1968 when its tacit support for de Gaulle's government helped the latter to survive against what had appeared to be overwhelming forces ranged against it.

The subsequent *mariage de convenance* with the Socialist party in 1972, called the *Programme commun de la gauche*, is described in the chapter devoted to the *Parti socialiste*, as is the demise of that programme. The victory of Mitterrand at the presidential elections of 1981, however, and the subsequent victory of the Socialists at the general elections, both with Communist support, saw a return to Communist participation in government. Mauroy's government of 1981 included four Communist ministers: Fiterman (transport), Ralite (health), Anicet Le Pors (civil service) and Rigout (continuing education and training). This Communist support had only been forthcoming, however, after it had become apparent after the first round of the presidential elections that Mitterrand was the only left-wing candidate capable of winning, and it had been preceded by Communist declarations that the Socialists were worse than the Right! It is not surprising, therefore, that this Communist participation in government lasted only as long as the Mauroy government and disappeared with it in 1984. After that, the Communist party went into a continuous decline, although it must be added that this process began in the late 1970s. Although it had more *députés* elected in 1978 than in 1973 (86 as compared with 73), this number then fell to 44 at the elections of 1981, to 35 at the elections of 1986, to 27 at the elections of 1988 and finally to 24 at the elections of 1993.

What are the reasons for this decline? The most obvious would appear to be that the French Communist party has experienced the same fate as that of the USSR and the other Eastern bloc countries. The growing realization in those countries that Communism had nothing more to offer – that it had replaced the oppression of man by man with oppression of man by the State, that its egalitarianism did not encourage aptitude and endeavour but levelled downwards, and that it did not create prosperity for all but poverty for all at the same time as it limited personal liberty – explains clearly enough why support for the party faded considerably. To these reasons, we could add that sociological and technological changes within France since the 1970s mean that the country is not nearly so neatly divided into the bourgeoisie and the working class as it used to be. Many members of the latter are no longer manual workers but skilled technicians working in specialized trades, or in 'white-collar' jobs, and as such belong to the socio-economic category which includes, according to Giscard d'Estaing, 'deux Français sur trois'. They are therefore more likely to vote for Centre or Centre-Left parties than for the old-fashioned Communist party with its image of *bals-musettes*, popular fêtes, accordion music and working-class culture.

It is also not fanciful to argue that as late as the 1960s Communism was not synonymous with oppression, for young people in particular, but with freedom. The 'freedom fighters' against the right-wing dictatorships in South America, Che Guevara at their head, were all Communist-inspired. Since the Russian invasion of Afghanistan, it could be argued, that view of Communism has disappeared amongst young people; the fight for freedom in recent years has not been in the name of Communism, but in the name of the struggle against Communism.

Finally, it has been claimed that the character and inflexibility of Georges Marchais, the general secretary from 1972 until 1994, is in large measure responsible for the lack of popularity of the party. He was perceived by many as a man who always took his orders from Moscow, who always pursued inflexible policies which allowed for little or no debate within the party and who was the main reason for leading young Communists with new ideas leaving the party – men such as Pierre Juquin in 1987. Marchais does not, of course, agree with the above interpretation and in his book *Démocratie*, published in 1990, he explains why. The following source text is taken from this work and from this the reader may perhaps judge.

Marchais was replaced by Robert Hue as party general secretary on 24 February 1994, subsequent to the Congress of the French Communist party. Whether this new appointment will bring about any major changes in the policies of the Communist party remains to be seen. Some new ideas have been mooted, such as the creation of eighteen *commissions nationales* to advise on matters such as the economy, social welfare, education, housing and the environment, and there is no doubt that Hue is in favour of these, but it is worthy of note that the six other members of the party's Secretariat are close associates of Marchais. This is not to suggest that there is conflict within the Communist party, and indeed Hue's convincing performances during the 1995 presidential campaign and his unexpectedly high score (8.69 per cent of the vote) show that he is very much in control of his party and that it would be premature to write the Communist party off as a totally spent force. Nevertheless, the 'municipal' elections of 1995 indicated that it still has the support of only approximately 10 per cent of voters and its leaders must be less than happy to realize that much of that support has gone to, of all parties, the *Front national*.

Sources

Extracts from Georges Marchais, *Démocratie* (Messidor, Editions sociales, 1990), pp. 36–45

Notre projet: de bout en bout 'à la française'

Cette place primordiale occupée par la liberté dans notre politique ne naît pas de rien, mais de ce que nous sommes: des fils et des filles d'un peuple qui s'est forgé une identité dont l'esprit démocratique est une pierre de touche. Communistes français, nous sommes d'abord des Français communistes. Rien n'est plus éloigné de notre démarche que l'idée d'un 'modèle' de société socialiste que les peuples n'auraient plus qu'à copier.

Cette notion a sans doute été la plus grande erreur du mouvement révolutionnaire mondial de ce siècle, qui a entraîné ses plus grands malheurs. Une erreur que le capitalisme, lui, s'est bien gardé de commettre! La Suède, la Turquie, l'Afrique du Sud, le Brésil, le Japon . . . Qu'ont-ils donc de commun, ces pays? Ils n'ont ni le même régime politique, ni le même niveau de développement, ni la même civilisation. Les différences entre leurs sociétés sont considérables. Et pourtant, ils sont, tous, capitalistes. Dans ces pays, comme dans les nombreux autres qui, sur les cinq continents, sont régis par ce système social, la classe dirigeante et son personnel politique ont appris à tenir compte de ce que sont leurs peuples pour les intégrer à la société d'exploitation. Ces peuples si divers – quelle faute d'avoir voulu l'ignorer! – ne pourront construire une société dans laquelle ils donneront toute leur mesure que si cette société est faite par eux et pour eux, si elle est à l'image de leurs personnalités, de leurs goûts, de leurs aspirations.

Voilà pourquoi notre politique et la perspective dans laquelle elle s'inscrit sont entièrement, de A à Z, construites à partir de la France telle qu'elle est et se transforme. Nous ne partons pas d'une 'idée générale' du socialisme que nous essayons d' 'appliquer' à la société française en 'tenant compte' des réalités de celle-ci: c'est l'examen sans a priori des problèmes tels qu'ils sont posés à notre peuple et à la France qui nous conduit à considérer que les bonnes réponses à ces problèmes sont des réponses anticapitalistes.

Dit autrement: l'ampleur et la profondeur des problèmes posés à notre société appellent des solutions précises. Eh bien, notre projet de société, c'est l'ensemble de ces solutions, l'ensemble de ces transformations qu'il est indispensable d'opérer pour surmonter les contradictions propres à la société française. On comprend pourquoi nous parlons de société socialiste originale, inédite, n'existant nulle part ailleurs, de **'socialisme à la française'**. Nous ne sommes pas prêts à renoncer à ces expressions, car elles font écho à notre conviction politique la plus fondamentale: c'est le développement même de la société française, **les obstacles qu'elle rencontre, les contradictions qui la minent**, qui appellent le dépassement du capitalisme; et la transformation socialiste de la France sera le déploiement de tous les potentiels de notre pays – de ce pays-là –, la création de notre peuple – de ce peuple-là.

Cela ne signifie pas qu'après avoir adoré dans le passé **l'icône du modèle unique de socialisme**, nous soyons devenus, par réaction, des chauvins indifférents à tout ce qui se passe hors de nos frontières. Nous examinons au contraire avec beaucoup d'attention les idées et les expériences des autres forces qui agissent pour le progrès de l'humanité. Nous apprenons. Et si nous découvrons chez ces forces quelque chose qui peut améliorer notre propre action ou notre propre projet, nous la leur empruntons. En matière de bonnes idées au service du combat libérateur des peuples, il n'y a pas de droits d'auteur qui tiennent . . .

Cela dit, j'insiste: c'est nous qui faisons le tri. Si nous intégrons telle ou telle idée à notre projet politique, c'est que nous pensons qu'elle 'colle' étroitement aux réalités françaises. Tel est, toujours et dans tous les cas, le seul critère. Pas de modèle, jamais plus de modèle . . .

Et les fameuses 'lois générales'?

Peut-être nous dira-t-on: 'Vous parlez de "socialisme original, inédit" . . . C'est à voir! Ce n'est pas en 1930, mais à votre dernier congrès, en décembre 1987, que vous avez défini "votre" socialisme de la manière suivante: **"l'appropriation par la société des grands moyens de production, d'échange et de financement,** une démocratie politique, un pouvoir représentatif du peuple favorisant à tous les niveaux l'intervention populaire, permettant à la classe ouvrière d'accéder aux responsabilités les plus élevées et d'exercer un rôle dirigeant". En fait d'originalité et de nouveauté, c'est la définition archi-classique d'un socialisme complètement démodé que vous voulez appliquer à la France . . .'

Je réponds d'abord en citant la phrase qui suit immédiatement ce texte: '**Notre conception du socialisme pour notre pays ne se réduit pas à ces transformations essentielles, mais elle les suppose.**' Il est, en effet, injuste de ne retenir de notre projet de société que ces seules caractéristiques: il en comprend d'autres.

Mais n'esquivons pas la question. Est-ce qu'en énumérant ces changements que nous proposons, nous plaquons une définition générale du socialisme, venue d'ailleurs et aujourd'hui dépassée, sur l'avenir que nous proposons à notre peuple? Non. Nous procédons par la démarche que je viens d'énoncer. Ce n'est pas parce que nous pensons que **l'appropriation sociale des leviers de l'économie** est une des conditions 'du' socialisme que nous la préconisons pour notre part; c'est parce que nous avons conscience du rôle déterminant que jouent les grandes sociétés privées dans notre économie et qu'il ne sera pas possible de changer celle-ci sans poser ce problème-là. Quelle ampleur, quel rôle, quel contenu, quelle forme doit avoir cette appropriation sociale, c'est une autre question que je traiterai plus loin. Mais que cette question se pose, c'est pour moi incontestable.

S'agit-il d'une exigence universelle, valable partout et en toute circonstance, sans laquelle la société nouvelle ne verrait tout simplement pas le jour? Ma foi, je ne vois pas bien comment une société pourrait se donner pour objectif de maîtriser son développement si son économie est dominée par les sociétés multinationales. Si on y parvenait quelque part, ce qui n'a jamais été le cas jusqu'ici, eh bien, je conviendrais que c'est possible, mais je ne pense pas que ce le soit. Ce n'est pas pour moi une question de dogme, mais de simple logique.

Déjà, en 1977, Jean Kanapa, qui fut l'ami le plus cher et le plus proche que j'ai perdu et dont la contribution à notre effort de renouvellement fut si riche, expliquait: 'Il existe des lois générales. Leur universalité tient à leur abstraction. Elles ne précèdent pas l'expérience, elles généralisent une expérience multiforme. A ce titre, elles sont historiquement relatives. C'est-à-dire, d'une part, qu'elles n'ont pas d'existence indépendante hors de la réalité concrète des luttes ouvrières, démocratiques, révolutionnaires; d'autre part, que plus l'expérience se diversifie et s'enrichit, plus le contenu de ces lois se relativise et plus de nouvelles lois s'ajoutent ou se substituent à d'anciennes.' Anciennes 'lois' qui disparaissent: Marx et Lénine avaient élevé la notion de dictature du prolétariat au rang de signe distinctif de toute position révolutionnaire; nous l'avons rejetée en 1976. Nouvelles exigences qui apparaissent: nous avons défini il y a plus de dix ans, en 1979, la démocratisation de toutes les sphères de la société comme une 'composante universelle du socialisme'. **L'évolution de notre propre réflexion et tout ce qui se passe à l'Est ont encore renforcé notre conviction que socialisme et démocratie sont inséparables.**

Notre but: libérer de l'exploitation, de l'oppression, de l'aliénation
Au fond, si nous devions aujourd'hui dégager les critères qui permettent de distinguer une société socialiste de toute autre société, je pense que nous devrions en revenir à ce qui est le plus fondamental. **Une société socialiste, c'est une société qui ne naît pas à partir de rien, mais qui succède à une autre.** Qui prolonge, donc, cette société antérieure en rejetant ce qui fait qu'elle est une société de classes antagonistes: l'exploitation de l'homme par l'homme et l'oppression de l'homme par l'homme. Le socialisme est la suppression de l'une et de l'autre. En Union soviétique, les travailleurs furent délivrés de l'exploitation capitaliste, mais pas de l'autoritarisme et de la bureaucratie. S'en libérer est actuellement la tâche principale des sociétés socialistes. N'en concluons pas pour autant au caractère secondaire de l'abolition de l'exploitation capitaliste.

On se dira peut-être que nous découvrons ces idées à la hâte, poussés par les événements de l'Est européen? Ce n'est pas le cas. 'L'expérience, avons-nous ainsi montré, prouve que les changements dans la propriété et à la direction de l'Etat ne suffisent pas à accomplir la transformation de la société. L'exploitation et l'oppression marquent toute la société capitaliste [. . .]. Une bureaucratie risque d'en remplacer une autre, des technocrates "de gauche" risquent de remplacer des technocrates "de droite". C'est pourquoi la transformation de la propriété ne saurait s'effectuer sans que soit entrepris en même temps un effort fondamental pour modifier les rapports sociaux.' Ce texte de notre parti date de . . . 1977.

Ce que nous voulons, ce qui fait de nous des 'communistes', c'est restituer aux êtres humains la maîtrise de tout ce qui dépend d'eux et dont les prive la domination des forces du capital, la nature de classe de la société; c'est mettre un terme à ce que Marx appelait 'le processus historique d'aliénation', qui instaure 'la soumission des personnes aux choses'. Car si on y réfléchit bien, les moyens de production et d'échange, les nouvelles technologies ne sont rien d'autre que de l'intelligence et du travail matérialisés; mais, devenus propriété de quelques-uns, ils sont de ce fait utilisés pour exploiter les salariés. L'Etat, c'est l'organisme par lequel les citoyens dirigent la société; mais, confisqué en quelques mains, il se retourne de ce fait contre eux et les domine comme s'il émanait d'une puissance qui leur serait extérieure.

Rendre ainsi aux individus le contrôle, la maîtrise de tout ce qui fait leur vie et dont ils sont aujourd'hui dépossédés, telle est la perspective de libération humaine qui est au cœur de notre combat. Entre l'être humain ou le profit comme but du développement social, nous choisissons sans hésiter l'être humain.

'L'œil de Moscou'?

En menant cette réflexion sur notre projet politique original, nous avons été conduits à affirmer avec toujours plus de force notre indépendance de pensée et d'action, qui est totale.

Comme on le sait, cela ne fut pas toujours le cas. J'ai indiqué qu'il était arrivé à notre parti de résister à la volonté de l'Internationale communiste. Il reste qu'il a longtemps défendu et respecté l'idée de la nécessité d'une ligne unique de l'ensemble du mouvement et de la prépondérance du Parti soviétique. Nous nous sommes, depuis longtemps maintenant, totalement débarrassés de cette conception.

Le premier acte qui le manifesta avec éclat fut sans doute notre condamnation, en 1968, de l'intervention militaire de l'Union soviétique et de ses alliés en Tchécoslovaquie, sous l'impulsion de Waldeck Rochet. Un an auparavant, celui-ci avait explicitement critiqué la notion de 'centre' du mouvement communiste international. Toutes les années qui suivirent nous permirent de souligner de manière de plus en plus résolue – comme je l'avais fait en 1973 dans *le Défi démocratique* – que 'nous définissons souverainement, en toute indépendance, notre politique, nos objectifs, nos méthodes d'action et que nous ne saurions tolérer aucune ingérence dans les affaires de notre parti, pas plus que dans celles de notre pays'.

Dire que cette conception était acceptée par les dirigeants soviétiques de l'époque serait masquer la réalité. J'ai encore en mémoire ce qu'il faut bien appeler un 'clash' que j'avais dû faire en 1976, à Berlin, lors d'une conférence internationale des partis communistes, pour y exiger que de nouveaux rapports s'établissent entre ces partis. La même année, notre 22ᵉ Congrès rendait publique l'existence d'une divergence entre le Parti communiste de l'Union soviétique et nous sur la question de 'la nécessité du développement de la démocratie et des libertés dans le socialisme', divergence si fondamentale que nous la faisions porter sur 'la conception que nous avons, les uns et les autres, du socialisme'.

Tout cela nous avait valu deux longues lettres de reproches en 1977: une du Parti communiste tchécoslovaque, et une du Parti communiste soviétique, qui demandait, en substance, à notre Comité central de se débarrasser de 'certains dirigeants', parmi lesquels il n'était pas difficile de reconnaître Georges Marchais . . . Le Comité central répondit aux dirigeants soviétiques comme il convient, et ceux-ci durent accepter, en 1980, d'établir des relations avec nous, après six années d'interruption, sur les seules bases que nous étions disposés à accepter: la reconnaissance de l'existence de désaccords sérieux entre nos deux partis, indépendants et égaux en droits.

J'ouvre une parenthèse. J'ai donc rencontré Léonide Brejnev une fois en six ans. Mais, pour nos adversaires, notre parti était à l'époque 'l'œil de Moscou'. Depuis le début de la perestroïka, il y a cinq ans, nous nous sommes vus, Mikhaïl Gorbatchev et moi, six fois. Mais il paraît que les rapports entre communistes français et soviétiques sont au plus mal . . . Ainsi va l'anticommunisme.

Aujourd'hui, les rapports entre les partis communistes sont fondés sur l'indépendance totale, le respect mutuel, la non-ingérence, la stricte égalité en droits, la reconnaissance, des différences et des divergences sur telle ou telle question, tous principes qui diffèrent radicalement de ceux du passé et doivent permettre à leur solidarité de se développer sur des bases saines.

Questions on the source text

1. What is the nature of the error which communism has made and capitalism has not, according to Marchais?

2. What do you think that Marchais means by *socialisme à la française*?
3. Marchais claims that capitalism is not suitable for France because of *les obstacles qu'elle rencontre, les contradictions qui la minent*. What do you think he understands by this?
4. Explain the meaning of *l'icône du modèle unique de socialisme*.
5. What is meant by *l'appropriation par la société des grands moyens de production, d'échange et de financement*?
6. What do you understand by Marchais's reply to criticisms: *Notre conception du socialisme pour notre pays ne se réduit pas à ces transformations essentielles, mais elle les suppose.*
7. Explain the meaning of *l'appropriation sociale des leviers de l'économie*.
8. Examine the reasons which lead Marchais to conclude that: *L'évolution de notre propre réflexion et tout ce qui se passe à l'Est ont encore renforcé notre conviction que socialisme et démocratie sont inséparables.*
9. What do you understand by Marchais's comment that: *Une société socialiste, c'est une société qui ne naît pas à partir de rien, mais qui succède à une autre.*
10. What makes a Communist, according to Marchais?
11. Marchais claims that the difference between French and Russian communism is enormous. Do you agree with his point of view?

Biography of Georges Marchais

Georges Marchais was born on 7 June 1920 at La Hoguette in the Calvados region of France. His father was a miner. He has been married twice and has four children. He was trained as a mechanic and worked in Germany in 1942–3, whether as a volunteer or as a conscripted member of the *Service de Travail obligatoire* (STO) is not entirely clear.

He has been a member of the French Communist party since 1947 and of the central committee and political bureau since 1959. He was appointed assistant general secretary in 1970 and general secretary in 1972. He has been a *député* (member of Parliament) in the Val de Marne since 1973, and stood in the first round of the presidential elections of 1981, when he obtained the excellent score of 15.48 per cent of the vote.

Over the last twenty years, his voice has been synonymous with that of the French Communist party and it has always seemed barely conceivable that he should retire whilst the party remains in existence. He decided, however, to resign his post in 1994, being replaced by Robert Hue, but has stated that he intends to remain politically active.

Long thought of as a hard-line, dyed-in-the-wool, obedient servant of Moscow and blamed by Mitterrand and others for the disintegration of the *Programme commun de gouvernement* which he signed with the Socialists in 1972, Marchais certainly appeared in the past to be in total favour of centralized State control and fervently against such dangerous innovations as Eurocommunism or *autogestion*. The reader will see, however, from the extract from his book *Démocratie* that he has come some way from those positions and that the present-day French Communist party, like the Socialist party, is saying that the basis of the Socialist ideal is not so much egalitarianism as freedom of the individual.

Whether this idea will continue to be stressed is unclear but Marchais has no doubt made the right decision to make way, at such an important moment in the development of communism, for a man who is less closely identified with the Soviet communism of the last twenty years.

Bibliography

Brunet, J.-P., *Histoire du PCF.* PUF, 1987.
Chevènement, J.-P., *Les Communistes, les Socialistes et les autres.* Aubier Montaigne, 1977.
Dreyfus, F.-G., *Histoire des gauches en France.* Grasset, 1975.
Fauvet, J., *Histoire du parti communiste.* Fayard, 1977.
Marchais, G., *Le Défi démocratique.* Grasset, 1973.
——, *Parlons franchement.* Grasset, 1977.
——, *L'Espoir au présent.* Messidor/Editions sociales, 1980.
——, *Démocratie.* Messidor/Editions sociales, 1990.
Programme commun de gouvernement. Editions sociales, 1972.
Roucaute, Y., *Le PCF et les sommets de l'Etat.* PUF, 1981.

See also the bibliographies to the other chapters, and particularly the one devoted to the trade unions.

6. Ecology parties in France

JUDITH K. PROUD

History and development

Since the foundation of *Les Amis de la Terre* in March 1971, the ecology movement in France has captured a great deal of popular attention both at home and abroad, not only for the progress it has made in municipal, regional and European elections, but also for its singular inability to make any impression on the composition of the French *Parlement*. A clue to the causes of this apparently paradoxical situation may be found, not only in the electoral system which the movement itself blames for its repeated failure to enter the hallowed portals of the Palais de Bourbon, but also in the nature of the movement itself, and, above all, in its inability to unite in one party, under one leadership, working towards a clear set of common aims.

Origins of the ecology movement in France

For the ecologists of the 1970s, life was much simpler than it is today. While a small minority came to the movement through a general ideological concern for the natural environment and the position of the individual in the face of increasing unbanization, the vast majority were inspired by individual, local issues. Whether it was the protection of a national park (Parc National de la Vanoise[1]), protest

---

[1] The first national park created in France (Alpes du Nord) in 1963. In 1969, a journalist at RTL, Jean Carlier, launched a successful campaign against the projected development of new ski runs in the park.

against a nuclear reactor (Fessenheim,[2] Bugey,[3] Plogoff,[4] Creys-Malville[5]) or outcry at industrial disaster (*Torrey Canyon*,[6] *Amoco Cadiz*[7]), activity was essentially restricted to within national frontiers, with most groups being created on a local basis, acting as *ad hoc* pressure groups. Where more permanent organizations did exist, they were still organized on a local or regional basis. The only group to have envisaged a more comprehensive structure was the *Réseau des Amis de la Terre*, created in 1977, which brought together regional groupings of the movement, which, having begun as a national organization, had tended to develop along regional rather than national lines.

This concentration on the regional dimension, and the relative success of the environmental lobby at this level, is explained not only by the local nature of the issues involved, but also by the electoral system most frequently used in municipal and regional elections. Proportional representation does not penalize smaller political groupings or pressure groups, and allows the election of lists of individuals who do not come from a strong party-political background. Growing popular support for the ecology movement in the 1970s was demonstrated not only by the increasing number of people attending rallies such as those held at Larzac to protest against the extension of a military camp,[8] but

---

[2] Alsace, 1971, 1,000 protesters; 1972, 10,000; May 1975, 15,000.

[3] Ain, 15 July 1971, 15,000 protesters.

[4] The one successful anti-nuclear demonstration; the decision to build a nuclear generator at Plogoff (Brittany) was cancelled by François Mitterrand.

[5] The first demonstration against the Super-Phénix fast-breeder nuclear reactor took place in July 1976 (20,000 people). The following year this was the site of violent clashes between demonstrators and riot police (31 July). One demonstrator was killed and 200 injured, several on both sides having to have limbs amputated as a result of the police use of grenades.

[6] On 18 March 1967, the *Torrey Canyon* oil-tanker sank, spilling 123,000 tonnes of oil onto 180 kilometres of coastline in England and France.

[7] On 16 March 1978, the Brittany coast was once again hit by pollution: 230,000 tonnes of oil from the stricken tanker polluted over 300km of coastline.

[8] This protest began in May 1971, when 1,000 people attended the demonstration. Six months later, in November, 6,000 people assembled in Larzac to protest against the plans, and in 1973 this number swelled to 60,000.

also by the results of the 1977 town council elections, which led to some thirty Green councillors taking up office. Contesting local elections on an *ad hoc* basis and under the auspices of, at best, a regional organization, was also particularly appealing to a large section of ecology sympathizers who rejected the kind of large, centralized and hierarchical party structure necessary to contest elections at national level.

The refusal to countenance the creation of a national party was indeed one of the most striking features of the ecology movement in the 1970s, and remains a bone of contention among supporters today. Ecologists argue that internal democracy suffers, as do the identity and rights of the individual, when subjected to the scale and rigidity of established party structures. Above all, the original policies on which a movement was based become submerged in the overwhelming aim of achieving electoral success once a movement sets its sights on national public office. Thus, when René Dumont contested the presidential elections in 1974 as the first ecology candidate on the national stage, he was supported only by a small *comité de soutien* which, although it enjoyed a brief life as the *Mouvement écologique* following the elections, soon lost momentum and collapsed.

Despite the ecologists' reservations, however, the need for a more co-ordinated approach to policy-making and organization began to make itself felt towards the end of the decade, not only through the actions of a minority of politically-minded agitators, but also through the changing nature of environmental concern. As the ecology movement gathered support, so the issues it covered expanded, to encompass such areas as anti-militarism, Third World economics and national defence policy. The geographical 'catchment area' of the ecologists also increased dramatically, moving, almost in one fell swoop, from the local region to the entire planet, as scientists warned of the finite quality of the earth's resources and the specific threats to certain aspects of the environment. The nuclear disaster at Chernobyl in 1986 only served to emphasize the global dimension of the environmental question. Such developments, whilst increasing national interest in the environment, tended to diffuse the previously concentrated attention of the ecologists, and also reduced the individual's capacity for direct action. This in turn highlighted the increased need for a national *political* party to co-ordinate policy and action, and above all to work towards electoral success in order to implement agreed policies at national and international levels. The need for such a national party was also emphasized by the unilateral efforts of a number of individuals or groups to contest the 1978 general election. The lack of co-ordination between these different campaigns not only produced very disappointing electoral results (see p. 139), but also led to overt wrangling between the different factions involved, which both confused and tarnished the image of the ecologists in the public eye.

Political parties

The first attempt to create a national organization in France that would concentrate on electoral politics was the *Mouvement d'écologie politique* founded in 1979 by the members of an existing Alsace-based faction, *Europe-écologie*. The move did not go unchallenged, however, and was considered by some to be highly schismatic. Certainly the MEP did not succeed in uniting all of the interested parties, a notable exception being the *Amis de la Terre*. The continuing disagreement among ecologists on the question of national party politics was further demonstrated only four months later by the creation of the *Confédération écologiste* which not only challenged the monopoly of the MEP at national level, but which stressed above all the importance of the regions in decision-making. The titles used to designate these different groupings also testify to the continued and deeply held mistrust of the political party amongst French ecologists, so it was even more significant that in 1982 the MEP took the step of changing its name to *Les Verts – parti écologiste*. The change in title was accompanied by an obvious effort to introduce a little more rigidity into the structure of the movement, but the overall organization of *Les Verts – pe* remained far removed from the hierarchical structure of the established parties. In place of a single leader, there were four *porte-parole* or spokespersons, and the regions retained a very strong influence in party policy-making. Such a move still failed to unite the ecology movement, and, only six months later, in May 1983, the *Confédération écologiste* also changed its name, to become *Les Verts – La Confédération écologiste*. Despite such an obvious attempt to muddy the waters, however, differences appeared to have been largely settled when, in 1984, the two groups merged to form *Les Verts – Confédération écologiste – Parti écologiste* (referred to henceforth as *Les Verts*), although some groups, including the *Amis de la Terre* still preferred to remain independent.

With the foundation of *Les Verts*, the ecology movement appeared, at last, to have created a national party to co-ordinate policy-making

and electoral strategy. Organized along the same lines as *Les Verts –
pe*, the structure and practices of the party remained highly democratic, and the regions retained a great deal of influence (see p.140,
extracts from Party statutes and the organization chart of party structure). These concessions to the anti-party phobia of many members
also struck a chord among the electorate, who, as the 1980s
progressed, were becoming increasingly disillusioned with the
choices offered by the established parties. The new party attracted
further favourable attention by maintaining an equal-opportunities
policy for selecting election candidates, and by suggesting that its
leadership had something different to offer from the professional and
jaded politicians of the older parties. The honeymoon period for the
new alliance was short-lived, however, for the ecology movement in
France remained fatally divided.

Brice Lalonde and Génération Ecologie

Despite the democratic ideals of the ecology movement and the
deliberate attempt to avoid the creation of individual demagogies,[9]
one character has dominated the popular perception in France of the
ecology movement. Candidate in the 1981 presidential elections,
Brice Lalonde benefited from the air-time accorded to all candidates
to put forward not only the precepts of the ecology movement but
also his own often forthright personality. Already known within the
movement for his *soixante-huitard* politics and his long involvement
in the Paris division of *Les Amis de la Terre*, Lalonde has, ironically, proved to be one of the most influential factors in sabotaging
the unity of the ecology movement in France. In 1984, when *Les
Verts* looked set to take a number of seats in the European elections,
which were held under a system of proportional representation,
Lalonde was one of the members of a rival ecology list, *Entente
Radical Ecologiste*, which effectively split the green vote. Further
damage was done in the 1986 general election when Lalonde set
himself against a popular candidate from *Les Verts* in the town of
Lyon, causing a reduction in popular support and again splitting the
ecology vote. Lalonde sowed further seeds of confusion amongst
environmental activists and supporters alike, when he accepted the

---

[9] Cf. the system of *porte-parole* introduced by *Les Verts*, and their insistence that members elected to office relinquish their post to the next person
on their electoral list half-way through their term of office.

post of environment minister in the government of Michel Rocard in 1988. This move was in direct contravention of the much-proclaimed independent stance of the party, which Lalonde himself had helped to establish with his 'ni droite–ni gauche' statement in an interview with *Le Point* in 1983. More recently, in 1990, Lalonde confirmed his rejection of *Les Verts* by founding a new ecology movement,[10] *Génération Ecologie*, thus apparently putting paid to any hopes of national unity among French ecologists.

Within the ranks of *Les Verts*, a number of individuals have reached relative eminence, either through their long association with the movement, or their election at European level. Perhaps the best known of these is Antoine Waechter, leader of the majority faction in the movement since 1986 and one of the many members to have come from the Alsace region. Waechter, an environmental biologist by training, lacks the flair and political expertise of the man known as 'Monsieur Ecologie', Lalonde. It is perhaps not surprising that many French people have not heard of Waechter, and believe Lalonde to be the leader of *Les Verts*!

Points of disagreement in political ecology

When the question of party representation at national level first arose, it appeared to be an issue that would cause irreparable damage within the ecology movement. Ironically, the divisions that exist within the ranks of ecologists who believe in the necessity of electoral aims and strategies may ultimately prove far more destructive. These divisions may be summarized by looking at the positions of *Les Verts* and *Génération Ecologie* on two fundamental areas of electoral strategy:

1. Political alliances

Les Verts: *Les Verts* maintain a strong ideological opposition to allying themselves with any other political party. In the current electoral system this means that a) they have little chance of forming a government; b) they will not work on the environment for any other government; c) they will not use their influential vote in the second round of elections to bargain for concessions on environmental matters.

---

[10] *Génération Ecologie* is not technically a political *party* in so far as it allows members to maintain or contract other party affiliations ('la double appartenance').

Génération Ecologie: Contrary to his early position, Brice Lalonde is now an exponent of the 'outstretched hand' approach as demonstrated by his acceptance of the environment portfolio under the Socialist government. Lalonde argues that this is currently the only way of achieving results. Opponents suggest that this is the way to fulfil personal ambition.

2. Political programme

Les Verts: They have had to formulate a comprehensive political programme following success in the European elections of 1989, and in response to popular criticism that they are nothing more than a single-issue pressure group. Because of their refusal to envisage parliamentary alliances, the party has to show that it is independently capable of government. Critics condemn their policies as idealistic and unworkable.

Génération Ecologie: They only have policies on the environment, which they seek to implement by whatever means possible, and as soon as possible, without waiting for ideal conditions (i.e. a Green government).

The way forward

The electoral strategies outlined above suggest that *Les Verts* are idealists, and *Génération Ecologie* pragmatists. Antoine Waechter has characterized their respective positions in terms of the two different courses of actions available when a bathtub overflows. Either you engage in a continual mopping-up process, the solution of Lalonde's party, or you turn off the tap. While Waechter's analogy is apparently logical, it overlooks the vital question of whether it is at all conceivable for *Les Verts* to 'turn off the tap' by forming a government.

Such an eventuality came one step nearer, in late 1992, when *Les Verts* and *Génération Ecologie* succeeded in burying their differences sufficiently to join together to produce a common electoral programme, under the banner *Entente des écologistes* in anticipation of the 1993 general election. This move was triggered by the regional elections of March 1992, in which both groups gained some 100 seats. In order to capitalize on this increased support, and to ensure that the ecology vote remained intact, the *Entente* formulated a joint policy statement (see Source Text and Questions), and arranged that only one ecology candidate was put forward in each constituency.

Despite great optimism on the part of the ecologists, and increasing unease on the part of the established parties, however, election results were devastating. Only two *Entente* candidates made it through to the second round; both subsequently failed to get elected.

The future

Les Verts were quick to blame the 1993 electoral set-back on the traditional scapegoats: the differences between the regional and the national context, the electoral system and – though Brice Lalonde and his supporters could not be blamed this time – the presence on the ballot paper of a number of 'pseudo-écologistes'. They are also eager to point out the advances that have been made by the ecology movement in the last few years, at least since the presidential election of 1988, in which Waechter polled 3.7 per cent). *Les Verts* point to the fact that the ecology vote has doubled in that period, and that whereas traditional strongholds like Alsace and Brittany have retained their Green colouring, other areas have begun to move in the same direction, most notably Corsica. The European Parliament is also held up as an example of the increasing support for, and power of, the movement, with 8 of the 29-strong Green deputation in Strasbourg coming from France.

As other parties continue to incorporate elements of Green policy into their manifestos, the future of an independent, political ecology movement in France remains unclear. In offering an alternative to the traditional party structures and agendas, *Les Verts* have certainly appealed to an element in French society disaffected by the increasingly traditional *alternance* between Left and Right, but the electoral system, their own divisions, and the contradictions inherent in their quest for electoral success have so far prevented them from achieving any marked or enduring success.

In the wake of the 1993 election defeat, the *Entente des écologistes* faces an uncertain future, but, as one alliance fades, others appear possible. At the annual party conference in Lille in November 1993, the anti-alliance policy so strongly advocated by Antoine Waechter was defeated by a majority of members. As a result, Waechter lost his dominant position in the party to Dominique Voynet, another member of the European Parliament and one of the only two members of *Les Verts* (both women) to reach the second round of the 1993 general election. Dominique Voynet was also their candidate in the 1995 presidential elections. She obtained 3.32 per cent of the vote in the first ballot. The possibility of future alliances with major political parties is now openly being discussed;[11] if this does not allow *Les Verts* to turn off the tap, it may at least help them to get into the bathroom.

Election results
(Source: *Les Verts* documentation)

1974 Presidential elections: René Dumont, 336,016 votes (1.3%).
1977 Municipal elections: 30 elected.
1978 General election: average vote of 4.4% in constituencies contested (168 out of 490). No members elected.
1979 European elections: *Europe Ecologie*, 890,722 votes (4.5%). No members elected.
1981 Presidential elections: Brice Lalonde, 1,118,232 votes (3.8%).
1983 Municipal elections: 300 elected.
1984 European elections: *Les Verts – Europe Ecologie*, 678,826 votes (3.4%). No members elected.
1985 Cantonal elections: no members elected.
1986 General election: *Avec les Verts pour l'écologie*, average of 2.44% in constituencies contested (28). No members elected.
1986 Regional elections: 3 elected (Waechter and Buchmann in Alsace, Anger in Basse-Normandie).
1988 Presidential election: Antoine Waechter, 1,146,000 votes (3.8%).
1988 Cantonal elections: improved results since 1985, but no members elected.
1989 Municipal elections: 600+ elected.
     European elections: *Les Verts – Europe Ecologie*, 9 elected.
1992 Cantonal elections: 1 elected.
     Regional elections: *Les Verts*, 100+ elected, *Génération Ecologie*, 100+ elected.
1993 General election: no members elected.
1995 Presidential elections: Dominique Voynet, 1,005,280 votes (3.32%).
     Municipal elections: *Verts*, 251 elected. Other ecologists: 379 elected.

---

[11] At the conference it was stated that '[Les Verts sont] ouverts à la discussion avec toutes les forces politiques et sociales, à l'exclusion de l'extrême droite, des ultralibéraux et des nationalistes' (*Le Monde*, 16 November 1993).

Extracts from the Statutes of *Les Verts*

Préambule
Compte tenu de l'expérience passée des mouvements écologistes, les adhérents aux présents statuts affirment leur accord avec les principes suivants:
- non double appartenance politique
- adhésion individuelle
- respect de la règle majoritaire avec droit à l'abstention pour les minorités
- autonomie politique
- parité des sexes pour les postes à responsabilité chaque fois qu'elle est possible
- instances nationales avec représentation majoritaire des régions.

Article 2: Les Verts ont pour but:
- de participer à la vie politique, en particulier de veiller à ce que l'expression propre des écologistes ne soit pas dénaturée
- de se doter d'une orientation générale contenue dans un texte d'orientation
- de débattre des alternatives possibles à la société actuelle, de proposer des projets en ce sens et d'œuvrer à leur réalisation en attachant une importance particulière aux transitions indispensables
- d'agir dans tous les domaines relevant de l'écologie, en particulier dans la recherche scientifique et médicale.

Article 3: Le siège social est fixé à Paris et peut, sur simple décision du CNIR, être transféré en tout autre lieu.

Article 5: Il [le 'parti ou groupement politique' "Les Verts"] est constitué de membres individuels adhérant simultanément à l'organisation nationale des Verts et à sa structure régionale. La structure régionale est composée de l'ensemble des adhérents de l'organisation relevant de la région, et d'eux seuls. Les Statuts éventuels de la structure régionale doivent être compatibles avec ceux de l'organisation nationale. En cas de contradiction ce sont les dispositions des statuts nationaux qui s'appliquent.

Article 8: La demande d'adhésion est reçue par une organisation régionale, qui délivre la carte d'adhérent, distribuée aux régions par le secrétariat national. Nul ne peut être membre dans plusieurs régions. [. . .].

Article 13: Un CNIR (Conseil National Inter-Régional) est élu pour un an. Il est l'instance dirigeante de la structure nationale des Verts entre deux Assemblées Générales dont il applique les décisions [. . .]. Il est composé:

- pour trois quarts, de délégués élus par les organisations régionales, au scrutin proportionnel de listes ordonnées, complètes ou non, avec vote préférentiel.

- pour un quart, de délégés élus, ainsi que leurs suppléants par l'Assemblée Générale au scrutin proportionnel de listes ordonnées, complètes ou non, avec vote préférentiel.

Les membres du CNIR sont rééligibles. Ils ne sont révocables que par une Assemblée Générale de la région dont ils sont issus. Dans ce cas, cette AG procède à la réelection de ses délégué(e)s au CNIR.

Pour être membre du CNIR, il faut être membre des Verts depuis au moins un an [. . .].

Le CNIR [. . .] fixe le nombre de délégués attribués à chaque région. Chaque région a, de droit, un délégué au CNIR. Le nombre des autres délégués de la région est proportionnel [. . .] au nombre de ses adhérents [. . .].

Le CNIR se réunit au moins une fois tous les trois mois [. . .].

[. . .].

Article 14: Le CNIR élit en son sein un Collège Exécutif d'au moins dix membres et d'au plus vingt qui comprend notamment le secrétaire, le trésorier, et les quatre porte-parole [. . .]. Le CE assure l'exécution des décisions du CNIR et des Assemblées Générales, et le fonctionnement régulier des Verts [. . .]. Ils [les membres du CE] assistent aux réunions du CNIR sans voter [. . .]. Ils sont révocables à tout moment par le CNIR. Les porte-parole ne sont révocables que pour faute grave. [. . .].

Article 15: Le Conseil Statuaire se compose de six membres titulaires et trois suppléants, renouvelés par tiers tous les ans par l'Assemblée Générale au scrutin uninominal majoritaire [. . .]. Ses membres ne peuvent détenir aucun autre mandat dans la structure nationale. Ils doivent être membre des Verts depuis au moins deux ans et appartenir à des régions différentes. [. . .]. Le CS veille au respect des statuts, de l'agrément intérieur, de toute décision du CNIR et du CE. Il peut

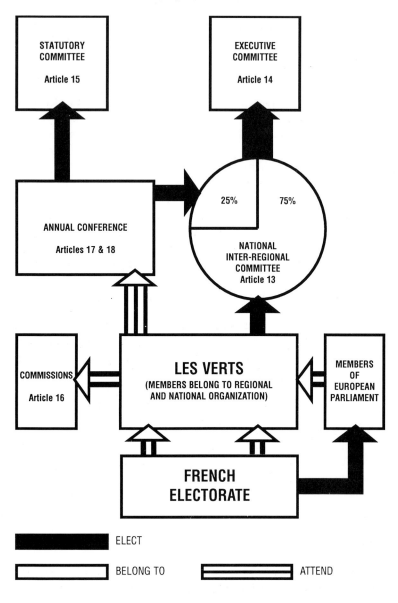

STATUTORY
COMMITTEE

Article 15

EXECUTIVE
COMMITTEE

Article 14

ANNUAL CONFERENCE

Articles 17 & 18

25%   75%

NATIONAL
INTER-REGIONAL
COMMITTEE
Article 13

COMMISSIONS

Article 16

LES VERTS
(MEMBERS BELONG TO REGIONAL
AND NATIONAL ORGANIZATION)

MEMBERS
OF
EUROPEAN
PARLIAMENT

**FRENCH
ELECTORATE**

ELECT

BELONG TO   ATTEND

LES VERTS
PARTY ORGANIZATION
(with reference to party statutes)

annuler toute délibération de tout organe des Verts pour non-conformité aux statuts ou aux agréments intérieurs nationaux ou régionaux. Il peut être saisi par tout membre des Verts [. . .].
[. . .].

Article 16: Des commissions peuvent être créées à l'initiative du CNIR ou sur proposition faite au CNIR. Tout membre des Verts peut participer à ces commissions. [. . .].

Article 17: Les Assemblées Générales se composent des seuls membres à jour de leur cotisation. [. . .].

Article 18: Une Assemblée Générale ordinaire se réunit une fois par an au cours du quatrième trimestre pour statuer notamment sur le rapport moral, présenté par le secrétaire, et le rapport financier, présenté par le trésorier. [. . .]. L'Assemblée Générale définit par le vote de motions les orientations politiques et stratégiques des Verts sur lesquelles le CNIF sera mandaté pour un an. [. . .].

Article 20: Dans tous les actes de fonctionnement des Verts, les adhérents des Verts peuvent faire appel à la formule dite 'référendum d'initiative militante'. Si le dixième au moins des adhérents, répartis équitablement dans le tiers des régions en fait la demande, une question précise est par voie de référendum posée à l'ensemble des Verts. Le référendum est organisé par le CNIR par l'intermédiaire du CE. Ses résultats sont décisionnels. Le CNIR peut prendre l'initiative d'un référendum auprès de ses adhérents.

Article 21: L'Agrément intérieur est élaboré par le CNIR. Il est destiné à fixer les divers points non prévus par les présents Statuts [. . .].

Source

Accord programmatique entre Les Verts et Génération Écologie (Élections législatives 93) [17 November 1992]

Nous avons une immense ambition: infléchir l'évolution actuelle des sociétés humaines, et inventer, avec audace et imagination, un futur qui ne laisse personne sur le bord de la route. Nous savons que les succès électoraux n'y suffiront pas. Mais nous sommes décidés à contribuer sans attendre à la résolution des problèmes majeurs auxquels l'humanité et la planète sont aujourd'hui confrontés.

Conscients de la gravité et de l'urgence de la crise écologique, de l'ampleur des remises en cause qui s'imposent, des réticences et des contradictions auxquelles nous aurons à faire face, nous sommes prêts à exercer des responsabilités à tous les niveaux, dans le respect des valeurs de solidarité et de démocratie qui sont les nôtres, en recherchant l'adhésion et le soutien de la population.

Le texte qui suit ne constitue pas un contrat de mariage entre organisations politiques. Il ne constitue pas non plus le projet politique exhaustif des écologistes, mais l'accord, à la fois réaliste et concret, sur lequel les Verts et Génération Ecologie s'engagent, à l'occasion des élections législatives de 1993, pour la prochaine législature. Outre l'adoption de mesures d'urgence indispensables et de propositions de caractère limité, mais significatives, cet accord affirme notre volonté d'infléchir les choix politiques sur le long terme, et fait des propositions novatrices dans cette perspective.

Les deux mouvements conviennent des propositions suivantes qu'ils défendront ensemble au cours de la prochaine législature:

1. la démocratisation de la société française

Les institutions de la Vème République ont été conçues pour assurer en toutes circonstances là primauté de l'exécutif au détriment du Parlement. L'Assemblée nationale n'est pas même maîtresse de son ordre du jour. Les collectivités territoriales reproduisent le même modèle avec les mêmes conséquences. Le maintien du scrutin majoritaire à deux tours, comme l'élection des sénateurs par les seuls grands électeurs, ne permettent pas une représentation équitable des différentes sensibilités politiques au Parlement. Ce phénomène contribue au discrédit de la classe politique, qui donne l'impression de fonctionner selon une logique qui lui est propre, s'éloignant chaque jour davantage des attentes des citoyens.

La démocratie de la société française passe d'abord par:

a. l'adoption d'un mode de scrutin qui assure une *représentation proportionnelle* de toutes les sensibilités politiques, accompagnée de la réforme constitutionnelle qui garantira le plein respect des droits du parlement et son indépendance par rapport à l'exécutif;

b. l'instauration du *référendum d'initiative populaire* au niveau local et du droit d'initiative législatif au niveau national, permettant le contrôle par le citoyen et, si besoin, la censure des décisions;

c. la poursuite de la *décentralisation*, axée sur l'extension des compétences des *régions* (avec un rééquilibrage des pouvoirs entre l'assemblée régionale et l'exécutif), et sur une réforme de l'organisation territoriale simplifiant et clarifiant les relations entre les différentes collectivités;

d. l'introduction du citoyen dans les processus de décision qui concourent à la *gestion du territoire* (élaboration des documents d'urbanisme, remembrement, infrastructures, plan de gestion des forêts publiques . . .); les plans d'occupation des sols devront être conformes aux schémas directeurs dont l'élaboration sera rendue obligatoire et aux directives régionales de planification territoriale élaborées par les régions;

e. la garantie des *droits fondamentaux* de chacune des personnes qui vivent dans notre pays permettant leur participation à la vie collective, économique, sociale, culturelle, politique . . . et l'exercice de leurs droits civiques;

f. l'adoption de mesures permettant une représentation plus équitable des *femmes* à tous les niveaux de responsabilité;

g. l'information des citoyens, base de tout *fonctionnement démocratique*, par la mise à disposition des dossiers, études, cahiers de délibérations, budgets, et de tout autre document administratif.

2. Une économie réconciliée
La tâche principale pour les prochaines années est de réconcilier l'économie avec les humains et la biosphère. Cette réconciliation passe par:

• l'acceptation des limites de notre planète;

• un ordre économique mondial, fondé sur des échanges équitables, qui permette l'amélioration des conditions et du niveau de vie des peuples du Sud;

• une maîtrise des consommations d'énergie, de matières premières, d'eau et d'espace dans les pays industrialisés.

Elle suppose de substituer des logiques de partage et de développement soutenable aux logiques de pure compétition et de fuite en avant.

Les premières démarches que nous promouvons s'inscrivent dans cet état d'esprit:

a. une politique volontariste de *déconcentration* des activités économiques et des créations d'emplois, qui limite la croissance des grandes *villes*, les concentrations humaines et la consommation de transports et remédie à la dévitalisation d'une partie du territoire;

b. la volonté de maîtriser la croissance et d'améliorer le fonctionnement des agglomérations (*déchets*, espaces naturels, urbanisme

. . .), et de redonner la priorité en ville aux piétons, aux cyclistes, et aux transports collectifs;

c. une nouvelle *politique agricole*, européenne et nationale, fondée sur le partage du droit à produire entre toutes les campagnes françaises et qui assure tout à la fois une production de qualité et un espace rural vivant: il faut sortir d'un productivisme ruineux pour les agriculteurs comme pour le milieu naturel; il s'agit d'adopter un système de prix et de soutien prenant en compte les données économiques et les exigences environnementales, ainsi que les services rendus au monde rural, tout en conservant aux agriculteurs leur statut de producteurs; en outre, les conventions de *gestion des espaces naturels* entre agriculteurs, syndicats de communes et départements seront généralisées dans le cadre d'un statut juridique et fiscal de la pluri-activité; afin d'assurer une solidarité entre le rural et l'urbain, la taxe professionnelle fera l'objet d'une péréquation intégrale départementale ou régionale;

d. la remise en cause fondamentale de la politique de l'emploi. L'échec des deux politiques suivies depuis 1973, tant par la droite que par la gauche est évident: le *chômage* ne disparaîtra ni par la relance économique, ni par le seul traitement social, ni par des rafistolages du système actuel. Dès lors, une profonde révision s'impose: dans tous les pays industriels, le chômage ne peut disparaître que par des changements structurels dans la manière de vivre et de produire fondée sur trois idées directrices:

1. la technologie moderne permet de produire les biens et services marchands avec de moins en moins de *travail*; la productivité progresse aujourd'hui plus vite que la consommation;

2. le temps d'emploi diminuera en même temps que le temps de formation augmentera, de sorte que la durée du travail doit désormais inclure la durée de la formation;

3. le secteur non-marchand, le tiers-secteur, le secteur associatif sans but lucratif, la demande de loisirs et de culture sont des domaines en expansion rapide, qui consommeront de plus en plus de temps dans notre vie.

C'est pourquoi les écologistes proposent quatre ruptures dans la politique de l'emploi:

1. *le droit à l'activité*, par-delà le droit à l'emploi, qui développe toutes les formes d'occupation et d'activité au-delà de l'emploi; encouragement du tiers-secteur, de **l'économie non-marchande**, du salariat

dans le secteur associatif, de **l'auto-production domestique**, du loisir culturel, etc. de façon à enrichir le temps de vivre autrement que par l'enrichissement en argent;

2. *le partage du travail*, en particulier, par le passage direct aux 35 heures, négocié secteur par secteur, sans perte de revenu pour les bas salaires;

3. *l'incitation au travail à temps partiel*, avec une indemnité de compensation pour les bas revenus, à condition qu'elle s'accompagne d'une embauche équivalente de chômeurs; Il s'agit de dépasser le temps partiel pour faciliter **la pluri-activité** et tous les rythmes possibles de travail, salarié et non-salarié;

4. *la gestion au niveau local*: c'est au niveau **des bassins de vie et d'emploi** que des solutions peuvent être trouvées. Il faut donc donner la priorité aux politiques locales de l'emploi, par une décentralisation massive des moyens disponibles;

e. une réforme en profondeur de **la protection sociale,** permettant un financement juste et pérenne de la solidarité: **unification des différents régimes**, association des usagers à la gestion des caisses, cotisations assises sur l'ensemble des revenus, l'objectif étant d'assumer la même protection à toute la population;

f. une logique d'internalisation des coûts sociaux et environnementaux dans le prix des produits manufacturés, soit par le biais de taxes, soit par l'obligation faite au producteur de neutraliser ces coûts;

g. mise en place d'une fiscalité écologique, taxant l'ensemble des ressources naturelles et des énergies non-renouvelables, ainsi que les activités polluantes, et affectant le produit de ces taxes à la promotion des économies d'énergie et à la modernisation des transports collectifs.

3. *Une gestion écologique des ressources et du territoire*

a. une **politique énergétique** qui se donne pour objectifs:
   – de se dégager à terme de la production électronucléaire dont chaque élément de la filière, de l'extraction du minerai à la gestion des déchets, soulève des problèmes non résolus,
   – de stabiliser les émissions de gaz à effet de serre;
   – de développer massivement le recours aux énergies renouvelables;

- de supprimer les incitations à la surconsommation d'énergie en particulier au chauffage électrique et à la climatisation.

Aucun nouveau réacteur nucléaire ne sera construit ou mis en service et **les tranches excédentaires** non justifiées par des besoins nationaux incluant des échanges techniques, seront mises en réserve.

La filière surgénératrice, ayant prouvé son inefficacité, sera abandonnée; une expertise indépendante des autorités nucléaires procédera à une évaluation économique et écologique de la filière du retraitement.

Dans le cadre de l'Agence Internationale de l'Energie Atomique, la France demandera l'abandon de la filière surgénératrice par tous les pays membres.

Le coût total du démantèlement des centrales nucléaires ainsi que les frais de recherche et de gestion des déchets radioactifs doivent dès maintenant être intégrés au prix du kWh vendu afin de ne pas reporter notre responsabilité sur les générations futures;

b. une politique d'aménagement du temps et de l'espace, des choix en matière de modes de *transport* qui permettent de stabiliser le trafic routier et aérien et de découpler le développement économique de la consommation de transports. Le programme autoroutier sera révisé à la baisse après une réévaluation par un collège d'experts indépendants, dans l'esprit de la Loi d'orientation des transports intérieurs (LOTI); les sections non justifiées et celles pour lesquelles existent des alternatives (mise à 2 x 2 voies du réseau existant, liaison ferroviaire . . . .) seront abandonnées; la modernisation du réseau ferroviaire devra assurer le développement du fer, notamment sur ses branches régionales et locales, et à réduire son impact sur l'environnement; le développement de transports urbains de proximité, économes en espace, non-polluants, est une priorité. Le transport routier des marchandises paiera son véritable coût; l'avantage fiscal accordé au gazole sera progressivement supprimé dans le cadre communautaire. La France agira au niveau européen pour la réduction de la taille et du poids des camions, pour que les nouvelles percées alpines et pyrénéennes soient ferroviaires, et pour le développement du **ferroutage**.

L'usage de la voie d'eau sera valorisé.

D'une manière générale les infrastructures économiquement injustifiées, écologiquement destructrices seront abandonnées (canal à grand gabarit Rhin-Rhône, barrages de la Loire . . .).

L'affirmation d'une priorité environnementale traduite au niveau gouvernemental par un ministère chargé de l'environnement, de l'urbanisme et de l'espace rural et disposant de moyens financiers conséquents (1% du budget dès la première année) et d'une administration territoriale effective. Les primes rattachées à la réalisation des travaux seront supprimées;

4. *un monde solidaire et pacifique*
Tirant toutes les conséquences stratégiques de la situation créée en *Europe* par la fin du communisme, le bouleversement des frontières à l'Est et la poursuite de la construction d'une Europe politique, la France proposera les moyens d'une *sécurité commune* à l'ensemble du continent européen, une stratégie ambitieuse d'aide au développement, la reconversion programmée de l'industrie d'armement et la renonciation au commerce des armes. Elle prendra des initiatives en faveur d'un processus collectif d'abandon de l'arme atomique, la première démarche de la France étant l'arrêt des *essais nucléaires* de Mururoa.

Au delà de ces points d'entente politique, les Verts et Génération Ecologie conviennent de poursuivre le dialogue au cours des prochaines semaines dans la perspective des élections législatives pour harmoniser leurs positions, notamment dans les domaines de l'éducation, de la formation, de la santé, de la justice, ainsi que de la fiscalité et des finances publiques. A cette fin, Génération Ecologie et les Verts mettent en place un groupe commun de réflexions et de propositions.

Questions on the source text

1. Explain the following expressions which are printed in bold in the text:

    (i)   *l'économie non-marchande*
    (ii)   *l'auto-production domestique*
    (iii)   *la pluri-activité*
    (iv)   *les bassins de vie et d'emploi*
    (v)   *la protection sociale*
    (vi)   *l'unification des différents régimes*
    (vii)   *une politique énergétique*
    (viii) *les tranches excédentaires*

    (ix) *la filière surgénératrice*
    (x) *le ferroutage*
2. What is the most immediate reason for this agreement between the Verts and Génération Ecologie?
3. How do the Verts/GE suggest the French people might be given more say in the way they are governed at local and national level?
4. Explain the terms *logiques de pure compétition et de fuite en avant* and suggest with which economic system they are most often associated.
5. What are the arguments in favour of the proposal contained in 2a, and some of the factors that might make it hard to implement.
6. Describe how three of the proposals listed in Section 2 *'Une économie reconciliée'* (a–g) directly affect the environment.
7. According to this document, what is the policy of the Verts/GE concerning:
    a) immigrants living in France
    b) the Third World.
8. What is the relationship between *le droit à l'activité* and the unemployment problem?
9. Explain the term *énergies renouvelables* and give both the English and French terms for two examples of such alternatives.
10. If the Verts/GE were to be elected, what would be the immediate effect on the price of electricity, and why?
11. Give details of three changes the Verts/GE would make concerning public/commercial transport.

Subjects for further discussion

1. Comment on the order in which the four main policy areas covered in this document are treated.
2. Discuss the importance of the regions and decentralization in the party structure and the policies of the Verts/GE.
3. According to the Verts/GE, 'Les institutions de la Vème République ont été conçues pour assurer en toutes circonstances la primauté de l'exécutif au détriment du Parlement.' From your studies, what evidence can you give either to support or to refute this assertion?
4. If you were a French voter, would this document influence your attitude towards the ecological movement in politics? Give your reasons.

5. What future do you see for this alliance between the Verts and Génération Ecologie?

Bibliography

Ecology newsletters

Vert Contact, national party newsletter, available from address on page 152 (weekly)
Verts Europe, Verts and the European Parliament, available from Verts Europe, 288 bvd St Germain, 75007 Paris (fortnightly)
Silence, 4 rue Bodin, 69001 Lyon (monthly)
Revue de presse verte, Groupe Vert du Parlement européen, from Verts Europe (see above) (25 issues since September 1989)
Ecologie politique, from Ecopresse, 62 bvd de Sébastopol, 75003 Paris (quarterly)
Combat Nature, from BP 3046, 24003 Périgueux Cedex 9 (quarterly)

Suggested reading

This is not a comprehensive list; many more titles are given in the 'Rapido' section of *Verts Europe* and in the bibliographies of the works listed.

Publications in French
Alphandéry, P., P. Bitoun, and Y. Dupont, *L'Equivoque écologique*, Editions La Découverte, 1992.
Bennahmias, J.-L., and A. Roche, *Des Verts de toutes les couleurs. Histoire et sociologie du mouvement écolo*. Albin Michel, 1991.
Brodhag, C., *Objectif terre. Les Verts, de l'écologie à la politique*, Editions du Félin, 1990.
Deléage, J.-P., *Histoire de l'écologie. Une science de l'homme et de la nature*. Editions La Découverte, 1991.
Journès, C., 'Les Ecologistes, l'Etat et les Partis' in O. Bacot et C. Journès (eds.), *Les Nouvelles Idéologies*. Presses Universitaires de Lyon, 1982.
Lipietz, A., *Vert espérance. L'avenir de l'écologie politique*. Editions La Découverte, 1993.
Pronier, R., and V. J. Le Seigneur, *Génération verte. Les*

écologistes en politique. Presses de la Renaissance, 1992.

Sainteny, G., *Les Verts* (Que Sais-je no. 2554). Presses Universitaires de France, 1991.

Les Verts, *Texte d'orientation*, 1983.

——, *Sauve qui peut la forêt*, 1985.

——, *Le Chômage: Partage du temps de travail et des revenus*, 1985.

——, *Le Choix de la vie* (1986 General Election Manifesto).

——, *Sortir du nucléaire*, 1987.

——, *Les Verts et l'Europe*, 1989.

Waechter, A., *Dessine-moi une planète*. Albin Michel, 1990.

Publications in English

Bridgeford, J., 'The Ecologist Movement and the French general elections 1978', *Parliamentary Affairs*, 1978.

Ellington, A., 'From pressure group to party, Les Amis de la Terre in the Paris municipal elections March 1977', MA thesis, University of London, June 1979.

McDonald, J. R., 'Environmental concern and the political process in France: patterns of the 1981 elections', *The Environmental Professional*, 1982.

Parkin, S., *Green Parties*. Heretic Books, 1989, pp. 89–109.

Further information may be obtained from:

Les Verts
50 rue Benoît-Malon
94250 Gentilly

Tel 010 33 1 49 08 91 31
Fax 010 33 1 49 08 97 44
Minitel 3614 LESVERTS

7. The trade unions

N. A. ADDINALL

History and development of the major unions

By their very nature, trade unions are pressure groups which represent the interests of their members. It is not surprising that some, in consequence, should represent the interests of the managerial class, and the majority the interests of the – broadly speaking – working class. For historical and numerical reasons, the text that we have chosen to illustrate this chapter is taken from the *Confédération générale du travail* (CGT) and it explains clearly the *raison d'être* of this trade union.

Before this, however, there follows an outline of the other major trade unions.

Confédération générale des cadres (CGC)

As its name indicates, this union represents the managers. It was created in October 1944, but changed its name to *Confédération française de l'encadrement de la Confédération générale des cadres* (CGC) in 1981.

Fédération de l'éducation nationale (FEN)

Created in 1928, this teachers' union is an amalgamation of more than thirty separate unions, including the primary-school teachers' union – *Syndicat national des instituteurs* (SNI) – and the secondary school teachers' union – *Syndicat national de l'enseignement secondaire* (SNES).

Confédération française des travailleurs chrétiens (CFTC)

Created in November 1919, this trade union, as its name indicates, was a Christian – or rather a Catholic – organization until 1964 when a majority decided to abandon its religious identity and become a trade union like the others. Thirty per cent of members decided, however, that they wished to keep their Catholic identity and these keep the CFTC in existence.

Confédération française démocratique du travail (CFDT)

As explained above, the CFDT was created in 1964 when a 70 per cent majority decided to leave the CFTC and its adherence to the Catholic Church and to form a new trade union. It has always been close to the right wing of the Socialist party and Michel Rocard in particular; like him it believes in *autogestion* (worker control) and the freedom of the individual rather than in centralized State control and egalitarianism.

Confédération générale du travail – Force ouvrière (CGT–FO)

Commonly known as *Force ouvrière*, this trade union was created on 19 December 1947 after a split with the Communist trade union, the CGT. In spite of its name, this union has very little in common with the CGT. It is very moderate and has many white-collar employees and civil servants among its members.

Confédération générale du travail (CGT)

The CGT is the largest trade union in France, and it is for this reason that, even though Communist-inspired and Communist-led, many non-Communists belong to it.

It was created in 1895 at the Congress of Limoges, and it has always made it clear, and particularly from its charter of Amiens in 1906, that in spite of its Communist preferences, it is entirely independent of the State and political parties. The following text illustrates this.

Sources

Text A: Extract from documentation published by the CGT subsequent to the forty-first Congress of 1982

Les caractéristiques de la CGT

L'histoire du mouvement ouvrier français a conféré à la C.G.T. une place originale. Cette originalité, la C.G.T. la manifeste en se définissant, elle-même, comme **une organisation de classe, de masse, indépendante et démocratique.** Chacune de ces caractéristiques mérite un approfondissement.

I. La C.G.T. est une organisation de classe

Lorsque des travailleurs se regroupent dans une organisation, ils entendent promouvoir la **défense des intérêts qui leur sont communs.** La communauté des intérêts des travailleurs se définit d'abord par le fait qu'ils sont **exploités** par des patrons (qui constituent la **classe des capitalistes**). L'exploitation est un rapport social qui conduit un groupe d'hommes détenteurs des moyens de production et d'échanges, à faire travailler, pour leur profit, un autre groupe d'hommes qui ne sont propriétaires de rien sauf de leur force de travail, qu'ils mettent à la disposition des capitalistes.

Le patronat a longtemps essayé de faire croire à une communauté d'intérêts des travailleurs et de leurs exploiteurs. Cette idée, qui a connu des fortunes concrètes diverses, notamment dans la France de PÉTAIN,[1] repose sur l'illusion d'une possible association du capital et du travail.

A l'intérieur d'une corporation donnée, ouvriers et patrons devraient mettre en commun l'intérêt de l'entreprise elle-même. La question: '**qui exploite qui?**' n'avait pas droit de cité dans cette conception.

Le syndicalisme de classe a été la réponse historique efficace à ces idées. Les patrons ont dû prendre acte de cette situation et se

---

[1] Pétain, Philippe, Marshal of France. 24 January 1856–23 July 1951. The hero of the battle of Verdun and its tragically misnamed *Chemin des Dames* (General Nivelle was the officer responsible for this offensive which caused the heaviest losses of the First World War, and he was replaced by Pétain). This well deserved prestige was unfortunately lost when he agreed to become the head of the French State by signing an armistice with the German invaders on 10 July 1940. The sentence of death declared on Pétain after the war was annulled by General de Gaulle, and Pétain died in the Ile d'Yeu, in captivity, in 1951.

sont, eux-mêmes, puissamment structurés en syndicat: le **CNPF**[2] assure la représentation des capitalistes.

La C.G.T., en se définissant comme organisation de classe, ne vise à rien d'autre qu'à affirmer le regroupement nécessaire des travailleurs dans une organisation qui prend en compte **la réalité de la division des classes dans le pays**. En mettant en commun leurs intérêts de travailleurs, ceux-ci affirment le caractère de classe de leur organisation.

Ayant mis en commun leurs intérêts d'exploités, les travailleurs engagent quotidiennement la lutte contre les multiples formes de l'exploitation. Ils agissent sur de nombreux terrains (pouvoir d'achat, retraites, Sécurité sociale, conditions de travail, d'hygiène, de sécurité, pour le droit d'expression dans l'entreprise, . . .) avec, en permanence, le souci de faire reculer l'exploitation. **La C.G.T. est donc, par nature, une organisation syndicale qui lutte sur le terrain de classe contre la volonté permanente d'exploitation des capitalistes.**

Elle se différencie en cela des organisations syndicales qui acceptent l'existence de l'exploitation et se bornent à proposer un aménagement du système ou, lorsqu'elles en demandent la transformation, ne mettent pas en œuvre une stratégie qui y conduit.

L'objectif ultime du mouvement syndical de classe, son but fondamental, ne peut être que la **fin de l'exploitation capitaliste et la libération, qui en découlera, de la classe ouvrière et de l'ensemble des salariés.**

II. La C.G.T. est une organisation de masse

'La C.G.T. groupe toutes les organisations rassemblant sans distinction d'opinions politiques, philosophiques et religieuses, les salariés conscients de la lutte à mener pour défendre leurs intérêts moraux et matériels, économiques et professionnels'. (*Article 1 des Statuts*).

En s'organisant dans la C.G.T., les travailleurs mettent en commun leurs intérêts de classe pour agir sur le terrain de la lutte des classes. Ils peuvent faire cela parce qu'ils ont, entre eux, une série de points communs dont le principal est leur **situation de salariés**. La grande diversité des salariés n'est pas un obstacle à leur regroupement dans une organisation syndicale de classe comme la C.G.T. Les différences de situation entre, par exemple, l'ingénieur

---

[2] Le CNPF (*Conseil national du patronat français*) was created in 1946 and represents businesses of all sizes and in every field.

de polytechnique[3] et le mineur de fond, l'O.S.[4] de l'automobile et le fonctionnaire des impôts, ne constituent pas des obstacles à leur regroupement syndical. La conception d'un syndicalisme catégoriel est étrangère à la C.G.T. On sait que d'autres organisations n'ont pas le même point de vue. La C.G.C. regroupe une partie des cadres et définit son action **en opposition avec les autres catégories de salariés.** Par contre, la C.G.T. fait de l'activité spécifique à l'égard des ingénieurs, cadres et techniciens, une composante de son activité générale. Elle a créé pour ce faire l'Union Générale des Ingénieurs, Cadres et Techniciens (UGICT).

La conception de classe articule du même geste la conception de masse. La C.G.T. ne pose qu'une condition à l'adhésion: **être salarié.** Une fois cette condition remplie, elle est très largement ouverte à tous, quels que soient leur sexe, leur race, leur nationalité, leur catégorie, leur croyance ou leur opinion politique.

III. La C.G.T. est une organisation indépendante et démocratique

Elle est indépendante du patronat et de l'Etat, des partis politiques, des organisations religieuses ou philosophiques.

Vis-à-vis du patronat, la chose est facilement compréhensible: on ne peut s'unir avec ceux que l'on est amené quotidiennement à combattre.

Vis-à-vis de l'Etat, si la C.G.T. ne peut être indifférente à la nature du pouvoir politique en place, elle se détermine toujours *en fonction des intérêts des travailleurs sur la base de son propre programme.*

La nature du pouvoir politique en place a des effets sur la forme et le contenu des luttes syndicales. Une politique réactionnaire s'attaquant aux acquis du mouvement ouvrier, mettant en œuvre une politique de casse industrielle, de chômage et d'inflation exige une action syndicale capable de mettre en échec le plus grand nombre possible des attaques et orientations développées.

Une politique affirmant des objectifs de sortie de la crise, alliant progrès social et efficacité économique, rencontre les préoccupations fondamentales de la C.G.T. Une telle situation crée des conditions nouvelles pour l'action syndicale: sans renoncer à ses orientations de lutte, notamment contre le patronat, la C.G.T. peut **se saisir du**

---

[3] L'Ecole Polytechnique was founded on 11 March 1794 under the name of Ecole centrale des travaux publics, the name being changed to Ecole Polytechnique on 1 September 1795.

[4] L'OS = *ouvrier spécialisé*. The name is misleading. It designates a semi-skilled worker as opposed to a skilled worker who is called *ouvrier qualifié*.

nouveau contexte pour renforcer avec les travailleurs son intervention dans le sens d'une pleine réalisation des objèctifs affirmés. **L'indépendance de la C.G.T. à l'égard des partis politiques est un trait original de la C.G.T.** Ce n'est pas le cas dans d'autres pays d'Europe, la Grande-Bretagne, par exemple, où le mouvement syndical des Trade-Unions a des liens organiques avec le Parti Travailliste. En France, les travailleurs ont des opinions, des croyances, des conceptions très diverses, ils font confiance à divers partis politiques, le pluralisme des opinions dans le pays se reflète naturellement dans la C.G.T., au plan politique comme sur les autres. En tant qu'organisation la C.G.T. **reconnait depuis longtemps le rôle et la vocation propre des formations politiques.** Elle reconnaît pleinement pour le présent et l'avenir, le **pluralisme des partis dans notre pays.** Elle assume sa vocation et conçoit ses rapports avec chacun d'entre-eux **à partir de son programme syndical.** Elle conserve, en toutes circonstances, sa liberté de jugement, de décision, d'avis et de critique qu'elle exerce avec le sens de ses responsabilités. Elle reconnaît le droit pour chacun de ses adhérents qui le souhaite d'être membre de l'organisation de son choix et d'y exercer les responsabilités qui lui sont confiées.[5]

Si la définition par l'organisation syndicale de ses orientations est au fondement de son indépendance, la démocratie syndicale en est la clé de voûte: l'élaboration du programme de la C.G.T. par les syndiqués eux-mêmes, réalisée au travers du Congrès, permet d'asseoir une mise en œuvre **démocratique** des orientations elles-mêmes **démocratiquement** élaborées.

IV. Le syndiqué et le syndicat

Les syndiqués sont à la source même du fonctionnement de l'organisation syndicale. Qui dit organisation dit responsables. Ce sont les syndiqués qui choisissent leurs responsables et les mandatent pour mettre en œuvre les orientations décidées en commun. **A la C.G.T. la notion de responsable incorpore la dimension du compte-rendu de mandat.** On n'élit pas quelqu'un pour un an, deux ans, trois ans, à une responsabilité qu'il assurerait seul, sans contrôle.

Non, les syndiqués investis de responsabilités par les membres du syndicat sont en permanence **responsables de leur activité** devant les différentes structures de l'organisation syndicale et, en dernière instance, devant les syndiqués eux-mêmes.

---

[5] The text points out clearly that the CGT is not attached to any political party and that members of all political persuasions are welcome. It is true, however, that it has a close relationship with the French Communist party.

A la C.G.T., chaque syndicat est maître de ses règles de fonctionnement, mais des principes communs peuvent être dégagés. L'Assemblée de base des syndiqués se réunit notamment avant chaque Congrès. C'est elle qui discute des différents rapports préparatoires, élit sa propre structure de direction, mandate ses représentants au Congrès de la structure supérieure.

Prenons l'exemple de la Fédération des P.T.T.[6]

1. le **Congrès départemental** est préparé par des **Assemblées des syndiqués** des sections de base (bureaux de poste, centres de tri, agences des télécommunications . . .): discussion des rapports présentés par les directions départementales sortantes, **élection des délégués** au Congrès départemental.

2. le Congrès départemental est constitué des **délégués élus par les Assemblées des sections de base.** Il poursuit la discussion des rapports et **élit la direction syndicale départementale.**

3. la même démarche est suivie pour la préparation du Congrès national de la Fédération: **discussion** des rapports par tous les syndiqués, **élection des délégués au Congrès national** par les syndicats départementaux.

Le Congrès national est constitué des délégués élus par les syndicats départementaux. **Il discute et arrête les orientations fédérales, il élit l'organisme de direction de la Fédération.**

Chacune des structures élues se réunit régulièrement pour régler l'ensemble des problèmes de la vie syndicale. Elles ont la responsabilité de la mise en œuvre des décisions prises après discussion. Hors période de convocation des congrès, les directions syndicales des différents niveaux de la C.G.T. doivent avoir pour souci de faire participer l'ensemble des syndiqués aux différents problèmes que rencontre quotidiennement l'activité syndicale.

Le rapport vivant du syndiqué au syndicat est une grande question qu'il faut s'attacher à faire vivre tous les jours. **A la C.G.T., les grandes décisions, les grandes orientations, les grands objectifs sont pris par les syndiqués ou leurs représentants élus (qui doivent rendre compte de leur mandat).**

Chacun peut faire part de son opinion qui peut être différente de celle d'un autre. *Il n'y a pas d'uniformité à la C.G.T., on débat, on s'explique, on argumente.* Il ressort, la plupart du temps, de ces

---

[6] PTT. Postes et Télécommunications.

échanges une position *unanime* des syndiqués, mais il est parfois des situations où l'unanimité peut ne pas se faire. Dans ce cas-là, ce sera l'opinion *de la majorité* qui prévaudra. **Si la décision suppose l'élaboration démocratique, elle ne peut être subordonnée à une règle d'unanimité.**

Ces principes qui régissent les rapports des syndiqués entre eux au sein de l'organisation sont à même de garantir un fonctionnement **démocratique et efficace** du syndicat. D'une certaine manière, on peut dire que la démocratie vivante suppose un double mouvement permanent: **du bas vers le haut et du haut vers le bas.** Chaque organisation, sous les formes adaptées à la profession, doit avoir pour souci de consulter ses syndiqués sur les problèmes importants du moment et de la période.

La consultation des syndiqués suppose que ceux-ci sont suffisamment **informés**, qu'ils ont entre les mains (et dans leur tête) les éléments du dossier sur lequel on les consulte. Des syndiqués nombreux, actifs, formés à la réflexion, aptes à apprécier une situation dans sa complexité, capables de discuter et de se déterminer font la force du syndicat. Cette conception du **syndiqué actif** est seule en mesure de donner **un sens plein à la démocratie**.

C'est par rapport à ces buts que la C.G.T. développe l'**éducation syndicale** et déploie de grands efforts pour la diffusion de **sa presse** (cf liste des publications de la C.G.T. in fine).

Text B: Extract from documentation published by the CGT subsequent to the forty-fourth Congress of 1992

(Text A dates from 1982. Have the growing economic pressures of recent years, the more widespread acceptance and recognition of the importance of market forces, even within the French Socialist party itself, brought about a relaxing of rigid positions, a willingness to show greater flexibility in relations with management and the private sector? Has the CGT, ever in the vanguard of the struggle against capitalism since its creation in 1895, changed, or at least modified some of its positions? Documentation emanating from its 44th Congress, held in January 1992, certainly uses a milder form of expression, but the same basic points about 'syndicalisme de classe', 'syndicalisme de masse' and 'syndicalisme indépendant et démocratique' are still clearly there, and even emphasized in the statement that the CGT may be 'indépendant' but certainly not 'neutre' in politics. The following extract from a document kindly provided by the Centre Confédéral d'Education Ouvrière of the CGT serves to illustrate this.)

Ce que se veut la CGT

• Syndicalisme de classe de par sa raison d'être, ses objectifs:
– un syndicat pour les revendications: il y a conflit permanent, fondamental, entre la logique du profit, de la rentabilité financière et les besoins sociaux.

Autrement dit, l'affrontement entre les salariés et le patronat, ou encore, entre les salariés et les forces du capital est constant. Ce constat historique montre que rien ne progresse pour les travailleurs sans leur mobilisation et leur action.

Cependant le syndicalisme de classe ne se résume pas à un syndicalisme de lutte. Il conjugue l'action pour les revendications et contre le critère du profit qui leur fait barrage: ce syndicalisme s'oppose aux rapports de production capitalistes. Il lutte donc pour transformer la société afin de répondre aux besoins, aux revendications, aux intérêts des salariés de manière durable.

La CGT est donc un syndicat de classe, parce qu'elle agit indissociablement pour:
* tourner l'économie vers la satisfaction des besoins,
* transformer la société pour répondre aux exigences légitimes des salariés.

• Syndicat de masse: tous les salariés créent des richesses ou y contribuent, qu'ils soient du privé ou du secteur public et nationalisé. Actifs, privés d'emploi ou retraités, à quelque catégorie qu'ils appartiennent, ils doivent ensemble, à partir de leur vécu, de leurs besoins, s'organiser, lutter pour que les atouts matériels, humains, culturels du pays ne soient plus bradés, pillés, mais au contraire, mis au service du progrès social.

• Syndicat indépendant par rapport au patronat, au 'politique' (pouvoir, partis . . .), aux conceptions philosophiques et religieuses, parce que ce sont les syndiqués qui élaborent, animent, font vivre les orientations de la CGT, parce que ce sont les salariés qui débattent, agissent, avec la CGT.

Indépendante la CGT? Oui! mais pas neutre, car 'la politique' intervient dans la prise en compte des besoins des salariés ou son refus. La CGT se mutilerait si elle refusait d'affirmer sur ces bases, des convergences, des divergences, des critiques sur les positions de tel parti ou gouvernement, à la lumière de ce que les salariés, les syndiqués ont élaboré au fil des luttes. Il en va de même des positions prises par toutes les organisations intervenant dans le champ d'intérêt des salariés.

• Syndicat démocratique parce que la CGT a le souci que chacun compte pour un, que chaque militant, chaque syndiqué, soit en capacité de participer à la définition des objectifs revendicatifs, tant dans leur contenu que dans la manière de les faire aboutir. Parce que tous les adhérents sont, à ce titre, responsables de la mise en œuvre des décisions prises. Cette volonté, elle la met au service des salariés pour qu'ils décident eux-mêmes de leurs revendications et de leurs luttes.

• Syndicat unitaire. Les salariés ont besoin de se rassembler autour des revendications et de réaliser l'unité la plus large, pour modifier, en leur faveur, le rapport de force, c'est un processus dans lequel peut s'insérer l'unité entre organisations à condition qu'elle ne se résume pas à un accord de sommet.

Il apparaît ainsi clairement que l'action pour la satisfaction des besoins des salariés implique une liaison étroite entre ces différentes notions, aucune ne pouvant être séparée des autres. Le syndicalisme de classe implique une conception de masse, l'indépendance, la démocratie et la volonté unitaire.

Questions on the source texts

1. How far would you agree with the definition of capitalism and capitalists given under section 1: *La CGT est une organisation de classe?*
2. Do you agree with the CGT's point of view that the association of capital and labour is an illusion?
3. What is the difference, according to the CGT, between itself and other trade unions?
4. What is the main point that members of the CGT have in common?
5. The CGT claims that it can represent the top engineer or tax inspector as well as the manual labourer. To what extent would you agree with this point of view?
6. Summarize the attitude of the CGT towards government. Does this show, as it claims, its independence towards political parties?
7. The CGT places much stress on democracy. What do you think it understands by this?
8. Do you see any major differences between the CGT and a large British trade union?

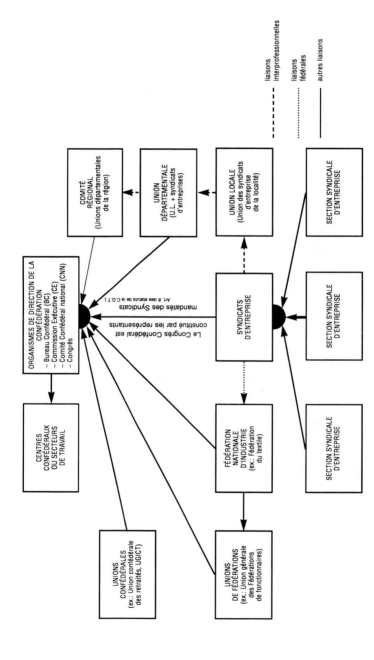

Simplified diagram of the structure of the CGT

COMITÉ RÉGIONAL (Unions départementales de la région)

UNION DÉPARTEMENTALE (U.L. + syndicats d'entreprises)

UNION LOCALE (Union des syndicats d'entreprise de la localité)

SECTION SYNDICALE D'ENTREPRISE

ORGANISMES DE DIRECTION DE LA CONFÉDÉRATION
– Bureau Confédéral (BC)
– Commission Exécutive (CE)
– Comité Confédéral national (CNN)
– Congrès

mandatés des Syndicats (Art. 8 des statuts de la C.G.T.)

Le Congrès Confédéral est constitué par les représentants

SYNDICATS D'ENTREPRISE

SECTION SYNDICALE D'ENTREPRISE

CENTRES CONFÉDÉRAUX OU SECTEURS DE TRAVAIL

FÉDÉRATION NATIONALE D'INDUSTRIE (ex.: Fédération du textile)

SECTION SYNDICALE D'ENTREPRISE

UNIONS CONFÉDÉRALES (ex.: Union confédérale des retraités, UGICT)

UNIONS DE FÉDÉRATIONS (ex.: Union générale des Fédérations de fonctionnaires)

- - - - - liaisons interprofessionnelles

· · · · · liaisons fédérales

——— autres liaisons

Bibliography

First and foremost, the magazines of the unions themselves, printed for distribution amongst their members, are good sources of information. The CGT's *Le Peuple* and *Vie ouvrière* are particularly well produced. Otherwise there are many books on the subject, of which the following will be found useful:

Branciard, H., *Syndicats et Partis*, Syros.
1. *Autonomie et indépendance*, 1982.
2. *Autonomie ou dépendance*, 1982.
Krasucki, H., *Un syndicat moderne? Oui!* Editions sociales, 1987.
Mouriaux, R., *Le Syndicalisme face à la crise*. Découverte, 1986.
Reynaud, J. D., *Les Syndicats, les patrons et l'Etat. Tendances de la négotiation collective en France*. Atelier, 1978.
Syndicats, organisations syndicales. Groupe liaisons, 1980.
Syndicats: Droit syndical, création, organisation, fonctionnement. Groupe liaisons, 1984.

Appendices

Appendix I: The presidents of the Fifth Republic

1. General Charles de Gaulle (22 November 1890–9 November 1970). President of the Republic from 21 December 1958 until his resignation on 28 April 1969.
2. Alain Poher (17 April 1909–). Twice provisional President of the Republic, the first time on the resignation of de Gaulle on 28 April 1969 until 19 June 1969, and the second time on the death of President Pompidou on 2 April 1974 until the election of Giscard d'Estaing on 19 May 1974. Poher was President of the Senate, and replacing the President of the Republic forms part of the duties of that office if the President should decease, resign, or be prevented from carrying out his functions.
3. Georges Pompidou (5 July 1911–2 April 1974). President of the Republic from 15 June 1969 until his untimely death.
4. Valéry Giscard d'Estaing (2 February 1926–). President of the Republic from 19 May 1974 until his defeat by François Mitterrand in the second ballot of the presidential election on 10 May 1981.
5. François Mitterrand (26 October 1916–). President of the Republic from 21 May 1981 until his retirement on the occasion of the presidential elections of April and May 1995, having been re-elected in the second ballot of the presidential elections on 8 May 1988 against Jacques Chirac.
6. Jacques Chirac (29 November 1932–). Elected President of the Republic on 7 May 1995, defeating Lionel Jospin (Socialist party) in the second ballot.

Appendix II: The prime ministers of the Fifth Republic

1. Michel Debré (15 January 1912–) from 8 January 1959 until 14 April 1962.
2. Georges Pompidou (5 July 1911–2 April 1974) from 14 April 1962 until 21 July 1968.
3. Maurice Couve de Murville (24 January 1907–) from 21 July 1968 until 16 June 1969.
4. Jacques Chaban-Delmas (7 March 1915–) from 20 June 1969 until 7 July 1972.
5. Pierre Messmer (20 March 1916–) from 7 July 1972 until 28 May 1974.
6. Jacques Chirac (29 November 1932–) from 28 May 1974 until his resignation on 25 August 1976.
7. Raymond Barre (12 April 1924–) from 27 August 1976 until 13 May 1981.
8. Pierre Mauroy (5 July 1928–) from 21 May 1981 until 19 July 1984.
9. Laurent Fabius (20 August 1946–) from 19 July 1984 until 20 March 1986.
10. Jacques Chirac (29 November 1932–). His second spell as Prime Minister was from 20 June 1986 to 12 May 1988. This period with a right-wing Prime Minister in government with a left-wing President (Mitterrand) has been commonly called one of 'cohabitation'.
11. Michel Rocard (23 August 1930–) from 12 May 1988 until 15 May 1991.
12. Edith Cresson (27 January 1934–) from 15 May 1991 until 2 April 1992.
13. Pierre Bérégovoy (23 December 1925–1 May 1993) from 2 April 1992 until 31 March 1993.
14. Edouard Balladur (2 May 1929–) from 31 March 1993 until 8 May 1995.
15. Alain Juppé (15 August 1945–) from 8 May 1995.

Appendix III: General election results 1958-1993

The elections of 23 and 30 November 1958 (*élections législatives*)
(major parties only)

Parties	First ballot	Second ballot
Communist party	3,882,204	3,833,418
SFIO (Socialist)	3,167,354	2,574,606
UNR	3,603,958	5,249,746
MRP	1,858,380	1,370,246
CNI	2,815,176	2,869,173

The elections of 18 and 25 November 1962 (*élections législatives*)
(major parties only)

Parties	First ballot	Second ballot
Communist party	4,003,553	3,195,763
SFIO (Socialist)	2,298,729	2,264,011
Radicals and Centre-Left	1,429,649	1,172,711
UNR–UDT	5,855,744	6,169,890
MRP	1,665,695	821,635
CNI	1,404,177	1,444,666

The elections of 5 and 12 March 1967 (*élections législatives*)
(major parties only)

Parties	First ballot	Second ballot
Communist party	5,039,032	3,998,790
FGDS (Socialists and Radicals)	4,244,110	4,505,329
UDR 5e	8,448,982	7,972,908
Centre démocrate	2,829,998	1,328,777

The elections of 23 and 30 June 1968 (*élections législatives*)
(major parties only)

Parties	First ballot	Second ballot
Communist party	4,434,832	2,935,775
FGDS	3,660,250	3,097,338
UDR	9,667,532	6,762,170
Progrès et démocratie moderne	2,289,849	1,141,305

The elections of 4 and 11 March 1973 (*élections législatives*)
(major parties only)

Parties	First ballot	Second ballot
Communist party	5,085,108	4,893,876
Socialist party	4,559,241	5,564,610
Réformateurs	2,979,781	1,631,978
URP–UDR	8,242,661	10,701,135

The elections of 12 and 19 March 1978 (*élections législatives*)
(major parties only)

Parties	First ballot	Second ballot
Communist party	5,870,402	4,744,868
Socialist party	6,451,151	7,212,916
RPR	6,462,462	6,651,756
UDF	6,128,849	5,907,603

The elections of 14 and 21 June 1981 (*élections législatives*)
(major parties only)

Parties	First ballot	Second ballot
Communist party	4,065,540	1,303,587
Socialist party + MRG	9,432,362	9,198,332
RPR	5,231,269	4,174,302
UDF	4,827,437	3,489,363

The elections of 16 March 1986 (*élections législatives*)
(major parties only). One ballot with proportional representation

Parties	Ballot result
Communist party	2,739,925
Socialist party	8,693,939
RPR	3,143,224
UDF	2,330,167
Front national	2,703,442

The elections of 5 and 12 June 1988 (*élections législatives*)
(major parties only)

Parties	First ballot	Second ballot
Communist party	2,765,761	695,569
Socialist party	8,493,702	9,198,778
RPR	4,687,047	4,688,493
UDF	4,519,459	4,299,370
Front national	2,359,528	216,704

The elections of 21 and 28 March 1993 (*élections législatives*)
(major parties only)

Parties	First ballot	Second ballot
Communist party	2,331,399	951,213
Socialist party	4,415,495	6,143,179
Ecologists	2,716,313	374,091
Union pour la France (UPF)		
i.e. RPR + UDF	10,074,796	11,347,846
Of which RPR	5,032,496	5,741,623
and UDF	4,731,013	5,178,039
Front national	3,152,543	1,168,160

Index

Action française 67
Aids 73, 77
Algeria 6–8, 35, 67, 68, 90
  Front de libération nationale 6
Algérie française, l' 7, 67, 68
Amis de la Terre 132, 134, 135
anti-Semitism 67, 68–9, 75
anticlericalism 2
Assemblée nationale 4, 8, 9, 11, 14,
  15, 16
austerity measures 30, 96
autogestion 98, 101–2, 118, 130, 154

Balladur, Edouard,
  policies 34, 53
  as presidential candidate 14, 32,
  37–8, 65
  as prime minister 14, 17, 166
Barre, Raymond 14, 30, 48, 64, 95,
  166
Bérégovoy, Pierre 14, 31, 98, 166
Blum, Léon 3, 101, 108
Bokassa, Emperor 30, 64
Bourgès-Maunoury 6

Cabinet, and president 10, 11
Cartel des Gauches 2, 120
Catholic Church 2, 68, 69, 71, 73,
  102, 154
Centre démocrate 48
Centre démocratie et progrès 48
Centre des démocrates sociaux (CDS)
  33, 48
Centre des nationaux
  indépendants (CNI) 67, 167
Centre national des indépendants
  et paysans (CNIP) 48
CGT *see Confédération générale du*

travail (CGT)
Chaban-Delmas, Jacques 13, 29, 35,
  50, 166
Charles X 1–2
Chevènement 95
Chirac, Jacques 35
  biography 45
  and *Front National* 72
  and Giscard 36, 63, 64, 65
  policies 11, 38, 39–45, 96
  as president 14, 17, 32, 34, 37–8,
  53, 99, 165
  as prime minister 11, 14, 30–1,
  96–7, 166
  and RPR 28, 29–30, 32, 36–9
  Discours pour la France à l'heure du
  choix 39–45
Clubs perspectives et réalités 48
cohabitation 11, 14, 17, 30, 31, 96–7,
  117, 166
Communism 2–3, 121–2
Communist party *see Parti communiste*
Comoros Islands 71
Confédération écologiste 134
Confédération française démocratique du
  travail (CFDT) 154
Confédération française des travailleurs
  chrétiens (CFTC) 154
Confédération générale des
  cadres (CGC) 153
Confédération générale du travail –
  Force ouvrière (CGT – FO) 154
Confédération générale du travail (CGT)
  153, 154–63
confiance 16
Conseil constitutionnel 12, 17–18
Conseil de la République (Fourth
  Republic) 8

Conseil économique et social 8, 17–18
Conseil supérieur de la magistrature 17
Conseils généraux de departement 10,
    18–19
Conseils municipaux 10, 18, 19
Conseils régionaux 18
*Convention des institutions
    républicaines* 100, 116
Coty, René 7
Couve de Murville, Maurice 13, 166
Cresson, Edith 14, 31, 98, 166

Daladier, Edouard 3
De Gaulle, Charles 29, 165
    and Algeria 7–8, 28
    and constitution 8–9, 12, 13
    death 29, 32, 35
    on defence 3–4
    policies 3–4, 32, 38–9, 96
    as president 13, 14, 29, 35
    as prime minister 7
    and UNR 28
De Villiers, Philippe 70
Debré, Michel 13, 166
décentralisation 18, 19, 29, 53, 95, 98,
    109
defence policy 3–4, 9, 11–12
Defferre, Gaston 103
Dumont, René 133
Duprat, François 68–9

ecology parties 131–51, 169
    local aspect 132–4
    origins 131–4
education 2, 69
elections,
    European 64, 65, 70, 139
    general 9, 16–17, 30, 31, 36, 95–6,
        98–9, 139, 167–9
    local 70, 71
    municipal 19, 69, 70, 71, 99, 139
    presidential 9, 10, 16–17, 49–50, 70,
        71, 94–5, 97, 98–9, 123, 135,
        139, 165
    regional 18, 65, 70, 139
    systems of 19–20
emergency powers 12, 23
Entente des écologistes 137–8
Entente Radical Ecologiste 135
European Monetary Union 53
European Parliament 138

Fabius, Laurent 14, 77, 96, 166
fascism 2, 3
Fédération d'action nationale

    et européenne (FANE) 69
*Fédération de la gauche démocrate
    et socialiste* (FGDS) 116
*Fédération de l'éducation
    nationale* (FEN) 153
Fédération des étudiants nationalistes
    (FEN) 68
*Fédération nationale des
    républicains indépendants* 48
Fifth Republic 7
    constitution 8–26
First Republic 1
Force ouvrière 154; see also *Front
    national*
Fourier, Charles 101
Fourth Republic 6–7, 8, 115–16
Franco-Prussian war 6
French Revolution 67, 99
French Socialist Party (SFIO) 3; *see
    also Parti socialiste* (PS)
Front national (FN) 32, 34, 75–6, 99,
    123, 169
    electoral success 69–73
    history and development 67–9
    programme 73–5, 76–89
    and UDF 49, 52, 69, 71
Front populaire government 3–4, 120

Gaillard, Félix 6
Galland, Yves 48
Gaullistes de gauche, les 28–9
Génération Ecologie 136, 137–9
Giscard d'Estaing, Louis 65
Giscard d'Estaing, Valéry 16
    biography 63–5
    on Centre Right coalition 49
    and Chirac 36, 63, 64, 65
    and de Gaulle 29
    and Mitterrand 30, 36, 94–5
    as president 14, 29, 35, 45, 165
    and UDF 29, 32, 47–9, 50
Démocratie française 47, 51, 52, 53–61
Deux Français sur trois 33–4, 51, 95
government, powers of 9, 14–15
Guadeloupe 18
Guesde, Jules 99
Guyane 18

Haute cour de justice 17
Hue, Robert 33, 98, 122–3

immigration 69, 72–3, 76
Indo-China 6, 90

Jaurès, Jean 3, 99, 110

Jeune Action,
    Fédération des étudiants national-
        istes (FEN) 68
    Occident 68
Jospin, Lionel 14, 34, 37–8, 95, 99,
    165
Joxe 95
Juppé, Alain 14, 65, 166
Juquin, Pierre 122

Lalonde, Brice 135–6, 137, 138
law and order 72, 73–4
Le Pen, Jean-Marie 32, 49, 68, 70,
    71–2, 73, 75
    biography 89–91
    L'alternative nationale 76–8, 79–86
    Pour la France 78–9
Lecanuet, Jean 47, 48
Léotard, François 48, 64, 65
Longuet, Gérard 48
Louis XIV 1
Louis XVIII 1
Louis-Philippe 2

Maastricht Treaty 37, 73, 85
Madelin, Alain 65
Marchais, Georges 121, 122
    biography 129–30
    Démocratie 122, 123–9, 130
Martinique 18
Massu, General 7
Mauroy, Pierre 14, 96, 103, 121, 166
Maurras, Charles 67
mayor, responsibilities 19
Méhaignerie, Pierre 48
Mendès-France, M. 6
Messmer, Pierre 13, 166
Millon, Charles 65
Mitterrand, François,
    biography 115–17
    and Chirac 45, 96–7
    and constitution 16, 17
    and Giscard 29, 30, 35, 36
    personal following 117
    as president 11, 14, 30–1, 45, 165
    Ici et maintenant 94, 99–105
Mollet, Guy 6
monarchy 1–2
motion de censure 15, 16
Mouvement d'écologie politique (MEP)
    134
Mouvement des radicaux de gauche 48
Mouvement républicain populaire
    (MRP) 6–7, 48
MRP see Mouvement républicain

populaire

Napoleon I (Napoleon Buonaparte) 1
Napoleon III 2
National Assembly see
    Assemblée nationale
nationalism 38, 67–8, 72–3; see also
    Front national (FN)
nationalization 32, 38–9, 52

oil prices 64
Ordre nouveau 68
Organisation de l'armée secrète (OAS)
    67, 75
overseas territories 10, 18

pacifism 3
Parlement 16; see also
    Assemblée nationale; Sénat
Parti communiste français, Le (PC) 4–5,
    28, 34, 49, 167, 168, 169
    and Front national 71, 72
    future 32–3, 99
    history and development 120–3
    and Parti socialiste 33, 94, 98, 99,
        116, 120, 121
Parti radical 3, 48
Parti républicain (PR) 29, 48
Parti socialiste (PS) 3, 28, 50, 167,
    168, 169
    and cohabitation 30–1
    and Front national 76
    history and development 94–9
    and Parti communiste 33, 94, 98, 99,
        116, 120, 121
    in power 30
    and social democracy 33, 34
Parti socialiste unifié (PSU) 116, 117
participation 32, 38–9, 45, 118
Pasqua 72
Pétain, Marshal 67, 155
Pflimlin, Pierre 6
pluralism 52
Poher, Alain 13–14, 165
Pompidou, Georges 13, 16, 29, 35, 49,
    165, 166
Poniatowski 52
Poujade, Pierre 67, 90
préférence nationale, la 73
president,
    and Cabinet 10, 11
    election of see elections
    independence 9, 17
    membership of political parties 13

powers 8–9, 12–13, 23, 97
and prime minister 10, 13–14
term of office 9–10, 16–17
prime minister, appointment of 10,
13–14, 30
privatization 37, 53, 74, 96
proportional representation 19, 32, 72,
132
protest groups 131–3
Proudhon, Pierre-Joseph 102

Rassemblement du peuple français
(RPF) 35, 36
Rassemblement pour la
République (RPR) 14, 33–4,
35–45, 99, 168, 169
and *Front National* 69, 71
history and development 28, 29–30,
35–8
principles and policies 31–2, 38–9
and UDF 31–2, 33–4, 50
referenda 8, 29, 73, 74
conditions for 11
Républicains indépendants 48
Réunion, Ile de la 18
revenu minimum d'insertion (RMI) 74,
81
Rocard, Michel 14, 31, 33, 34, 96,
98–9, 116, 117, 136, 154, 166
biography 117–18
Un pays comme le nôtre 105–12
Rossinot, André 48
Rousseau, Jean-Jacques 1

St Pierre et Miquelon (*département*) 18
salaire minimum interprofessionnel
de croissance (SMIC) 74
Savary, Alain 103
scandal 30, 64
Second Republic 2
Seguin, Philippe 36–7
Sénat 16; *see also Assemblée*
nationale; Parlement
Servan-Schreiber, Jean-Jacques 48, 64
social democracy 33, 34, 48, 98–9,
105–12, 114–15, 118
Socialist party *see Parti socialiste*
Soustelle, Jacques 6
sovereignty 32, 38
Stirbois, Jean-Pierre 69
Suarez 1
subsidiarity 53

Third Republic 2, 4
Thorez, Maurice 120, 121
Tibéri, Jean 45
Tixier-Vignancourt, Jean-Louis 68, 90
trade unions 74
Confédération générale du
travail (CGT) 153, 154–63
history and development 153–4

UDF *see Union pour la*
démocratie française
Union de défense des commerçants
et artisans (UDCA) 67, 90
Union des démocrates pour
la République (UDR) 36
Union des démocrates pour la
Ve République (UDR 5e) 36
Union pour la défense de la République
36
Union pour la démocratie
française (UDF) 29, 30, 31–2,
33–4, 53–65, 168, 169
in elections 49–50
and *Front national* 49, 52, 69, 71
history and development 47–9
principles and policies 51–3
Union pour la Nouvelle République
(UNR) 13, 28–9, 36, 167
Union pour la Nouvelle
République–Union démocrate du
travail (UNR–UDT) 36, 167
UNR *see Union pour la*
Nouvelle République
USSR 120, 121–2

Verts, Les – Confédération écologiste –
Parti écologiste (Les Verts) 134–6,
138–9
political alliances 136, 138–9
political programme 137
Verts, Les – La Confédération
écologiste 134
Verts, Les – parti écologiste 134
Vichy government 4, 67, 155
violence 67, 68, 75
Voynet, Dominique 138–9

Waechter, Antoine 136, 137, 138
Waldeck-Rochet 121
Weil, Simone 65
World War One 2, 3
World War Two 4